MW01120174

All Things Possible

Linotte Joseph
with Cullen Vane

T & Z Publishing

All Things Possible

T & Z Publishing
Roseville, West Palm Beach, Carries

Cover photographs: Sarah Dolan
Photograph editing: Lori Lynn Lisa

ISBN-13: 978-1530831975
ISBN-10: 1530831970

For the glory of God.

For my mother, Fernesia, who has been a rock.
For my husband, Jean Claude Joseph.
For my children: Don, Rick, Luc, Edwin, Brian and Elizabeth.
For my brothers: Luckner, Claude, Jocelyn and Jonas.
For Grace Community Christian Church of Boca Raton who are my family united by the blood of Jesus Christ.
To Miss Kim, thank you for believing in me.
For my friend, Violet Benoit, who has never stopped praying for me.
To Manassé Dorival, who always encourages and supports this journey.
To Miss Doodle and her husband, Mike, for being pillars to this community.

For all of the individuals who live in the Mission of Grace.
For all of the individuals who work for the Mission of Grace.
For all of the individuals who love the Mission of Grace.

† † †

For Tyler and Zachary
For those of The Rock of Roseville

FOREWARD
Miriam "Doodle" Cinotti

From the moment we met Miss Lynn it seemed as if our hearts and minds were knitted together. It was our first mission trip to Haiti and we've been back more than twenty times and each time we'll sit and listen to what God has put in her heart. She has so much love for the people she serves that you can't help but want to be a part of her mission with God leading the way.

During our second trip to Haiti, Miss Lynn was showing up around Carries and was explaining how the village needed a focal point, something to draw people together. It didn't seem like that big of a vision and so we claimed the land, prayed over it, and it was a matter of months before we'd procured funding and had missionary teams building walls. That building is a church, but it is also used for a school and has been used for a clinic. Weddings and funerals have been performed within. Bible studies take place there every week. It has been used for community meetings. It isn't just a focal point, it is a beacon on the hill with love pouring out over the people of the village. Just that one project has meant so much that it's nearly impossible to imagine the village without it. There are other churches in the village, but none had taken up the mantle to be a community leader.

Miss Lynn's vision of a "focal point" has turned into just that, and though many have ideas but few are those who have the wisdom to see them through to completion.

What has happened in Carries over the past six years is amazing. The people are cleaner, healthier and better educated. There are jobs being created and when people see success it's infectious. By obeying God, even when it was difficult to do so, Miss Lynn blazed a trail so the lives of many others could be better than they were. I don't know if there's a higher purpose in one's life.

We of Team Haiti love serving the Mission of Grace and our blessings for doing so are twenty-fold what we've put in.

Mike and Doodle Cinotti
Team Haiti
Southpoint Community Church

PROLOGUE

The complete story of the mission described in this book cannot be fully put onto paper. Even I, who have been here since the beginning and have experienced its highs and lows, its successes and disappointments, do not know the whole story and am not entirely aware of what the mission is and what it does. It is too big for any one person to know.

So much has happened in these past six years and so many people have come and gone that I couldn't possibly recall or thank them all. In the process of writing this book I've had the opportunity to look back and it's only on reflection that I realized that several hundred people have been part of the mission. The vines of what we've become are ever reaching and our family is very large and growing.

Not all of the stories, nor all of the people behind the stories, made it into this book and I mean no slight to those not mentioned or to those who might merit more credit than I give them. I am forever grateful for every single person who has had even the smallest hand in making the mission a success. Although I am, in many respects, the face of the mission, it certainly is not about me, it is all about God and He knows the roles many have played, whether named here or not and whether they are given the recognition they might deserve.

Something great is happening in the village of Carries, a place that is as much a character in this book as any person. It is also a place where greatness has been a foreign concept and hope was just a dream. However, dreams sometimes do come true and it is our hope that *in* the greatness of what Carries is becoming, people will prosper.

From day one, the mission has been to create servants in Jesus' vision for the benefit of Haiti and to expand the kingdom of God to benefit all. Those are worthy objectives, though not always easy to achieve. But anything worth doing is worth slogging through the mess to accomplish, and no matter how many times we fall, or how many times we stray from our appointment, God stands beside us to correct our path and to lead us through dark waters with the light of faith, hope and love.

Linotte Joseph
Carries, Haiti

All Things Possible

Haiti

ONE
An Unnecessary Death

Her name was Masaline and her death wasn't expected, nor was it unexpected. Some lived and some died, that's the way it had always been, whether needful or not. In a little village, far from any medical facilities and a lonely outpost for 8,000 people who struggled each day for sustenance, another death was routine. Assuredly, the news was given thought, there was sadness and wailing, and prayers were said, but it couldn't be dwelt on for long because tomorrow would soon arrive and those living would have to continue to find a way to do so.

At that time, death was a cheap commodity in the small village of Carries [Car-ee-ess], although it was not alone in Haiti where death has always been a cheap commodity. For hundreds of years death had been doled out for any number of reasons and in any number of ways, few of which made sense especially in a modern era when much of the world had the means to stomp out at least some of the random deaths. But the modern world hadn't caught up to Carries and the village had an unsure footing in the 21st Century and seemed, in many respects, to be shackled to a much earlier time.

However, sometimes all it takes is one death to wake the conscience and to exert change. Sometimes it takes only one person to break the dam that allows water to run freely, a person like Jesus, perhaps, or even someone without godly powers but has God on their side. A person who believes that with God, all things are possible.

TWO
A Woman of Two Countries

I am Haitian and I have never turned my back on that fact. Boldly I proclaim my roots because it is who I am, but as a young woman of nineteen I left my native country for the United States and for more than thirty years I had no intention of *ever* making Haiti my permanent home again. However, as He often does, God had other ideas.

In 2009, as I reached my 50s, my children were grown and I was living very comfortably in Florida. Life was good except for the periodic illnesses and maladies that would overtake me and leave me debilitated, none of which could be explained. I saw a slew of doctors and experts, I stayed at the best hospitals, I was poked, prodded and probed until I was sore, I had every test under the sun performed on me and everyone told me I was alright, but they were wrong. I was *not* alright but no doctor could find the source of my problems. It's more than a little frustrating when so-called "experts" use all of their expertise only to come up with nothing and I was left in a malaise from a disorder that no one could name.

I tried to work through the aches and pains until I could stand them no longer and then it would be off to see even more doctors who would also tell me there was nothing wrong with me, something I knew was incorrect because I was often weakened and was sometimes forced to just lie on the couch in the dark.

Since nothing wrong could be found with me *physically*, some suggested that it might be a mental problem I was suffering from and so I saw even more experts, psychiatrists and psychologists, who studied me and gave me more tests, but none could come up with a definitive answer as to what my problem might be and nothing was solved. One doctor thought I might be suffering from anxiety, though for *what* he couldn't say, and so I was prescribed Xanax, but that didn't do even one bit of good. *Nothing* did any good except to close myself up in my house and pray that the day would end and that in the morning my world would be right again, but it never was.

It was maddening that for months and months I simply could not get well—except, amazingly enough, when I periodically returned to Haiti.

I had often gone back and forth between my two countries, spending time in Haiti when I wanted to, most often for family reasons. My husband and I have kept a house and property in Pétion-Ville, a suburb of Port-au-Prince, and for more than twenty years the family has owned a little property up the coast from the capital that included a beach house that offered refuge for me and my family from our often chaotic lives. In

2009 we turned the property into a small resort called Ocean View that sits on the beach at the little village named Carries.

THREE
A Village

Carries is a place that few Haitians, and fewer non-Haitians, have ever heard about, and certainly fewer in 2009 than today. It was a place that one did not go to unless they had a reason, and there are very few reasons to go. To get there one must take Haiti's National Route 1 from the International Airport in Port-au-Prince and head north. Once out of the chaos and bedlam of the capital, it is a pleasant drive as the landscape opens up from the chaos into the leisurely and rather serene pace found outside.

The landscape along the western edge of the country gradually forces the road to skirt the mountains so that by the time it reaches Carries it has been thrust toward the ocean and only a sliver of land a few hundred feet wide separates the highway from the water.

At Carries, on the inland side of the highway, the rugged and rocky slopes of the *Chaîne des Matheux* start to rise from the village proper. On the ocean side of the highway are many lavish homes and several resorts that course the sandy beaches, including Ocean View.

To say that Carries is poor would be an under-statement. To say that its people are poor of spirit would be a falsehood. The people of Carries lack material wealth, and are oftentimes hungry, but they have a spirit that is of wealth and is of the sort that even a rich person cannot buy. Carries is a wonderful place although its wonders have only begun to be uncovered.

In 2009, when my story begins, Carries was a place simply because it had a collection of people and housing of the most basic sort. Most residents lived in dirt-floor shacks cobbled together with fragments of wood and corrugated metal, cardboard, plastic or scraps of any sort. Those who were better off had homes made of cinderblocks that were often finished off with a concrete sluice on the outside walls. Unlike in large cities where shanties are placed so closely together that it is difficult for a rat to squeeze between, there is enough land that houses most often have a yard where crops could be wheedled, if such a thing were possible in such uninviting soil, which it is not.

The roads in Carries meander this way and that, uphill and downhill, and were carved underfoot. The village had no plan when it was created, it was just where people stopped and it grew in a hodge-podge manner. The roads aren't really *roads* but rocky trails that are hard to traverse especially when carrying a bucket or a bundle on one's head.

Aside from people and shanties there was nothing, really, that would designate it *as* a "place." It had people, perhaps 7,000 in total, spread out over a wide and ugly piece of rocky and turbulent terrain, and it had some goats and chickens and even a cow or two, although they tended to be about the ugliest cows one had ever laid eyes upon.

Carries had few assets then – its people and a beautiful view of the ocean, and besides those it was just a place with no cause, rhyme or reason for its existence.

What it did not have were the basic services many consider essential in modern times. It did not have sewers, running water, stores (because no one has money to spend in stores) or a government, and without a government there are no taxes collected and with no taxes collected there are no government services. There were no petrol stations or toilet facilities except holes in the ground that are given the barest privacy by flimsy structures built around them. It had no cars, a few motorcycles, no internet or cellphone service (except at the resorts), no electricity (except at the resorts), no social services, certainly no bank, no doctors and no nurses. There was no sign that said "Welcome to Carries" and by the time someone might know they were passing through on the highway they had already left it behind.

If there is a history to Carries no one knows what it is because it most certainly is not recorded. What is known about Carries' history is this; that it has been there for longer than anyone alive can remember. As no one famous has ever been born in the village, and no one famous has died in the village, and no revolutionary activity has ever occurred in the village, then it is a no place for most Haitians and certainly for the government that didn't even know it existed.

Carries is important to my story because it is as much a character as any person and because it is where God sent me to be. To not have at least a general understanding of what type of place it was, and is, and what it can someday *be*, is to not give it the justice it deserves. In getting sent there, others have followed, and I know they've been sent by God as well.

FOUR
No Desire to go Home

My husband, Jean Claude, is a strong and sweet man who does not waste words and carries himself better than most without even trying. He is quiet while I am loud. He is reserved while I am brash. As I was going through my many sicknesses that had no answers, every time we visited Haiti the illness would slowly recede and then go away completely. And as I would be getting better in my native home, Jean Claude would often say to me, "God is telling me that He is calling you back to Haiti."

"Why is God telling *you* and not *me*?" I'd ask with annoyance. "If God wants me to stay so badly, tell him to talk to *me*!"

Even though it seemed as if it was the *place* itself that was the cure for whatever my ailments were, I never had any intention of staying in Haiti except for short visits. My husband could have told me a thousand times that *there* is where I was supposed to be, but I am sometimes, maybe oftentimes, stubborn. For what reason would I want or need to leave my comfortable life in Florida for a place that always seemed to be on the verge of chaos, as Haiti is? I was only too aware of Haiti's worst elements and had long tried to avoid those features. And even though my husband kept telling me over and over that he'd been told by *God* that Haiti was where I was supposed to be, I did not listen. And on reflection, perhaps it wasn't only my husband I wasn't listening to, but also God himself.

I should have trusted my husband's wisdom instead of sticking to my own stubbornness. But it's funny, or ironic, or perhaps sad, that even without getting prodded by my husband, I *knew* there was something lacking in my life and I had the sneaking suspicion, deep in the back of my brain, that whatever it was could *only* be found in Haiti. I was feeling a pull, though from what, where or who, I did not know. It is always easy to see in hindsight, to understand from a perspective of looking back, and now I can see how the Hand of God was at play although I did not see it then and little did I show that I was an obedient servant.

I'd been raised in the Baptist church by my parents who were God-fearing and God loving, and they had raised me to do right and be right with God. At an early age I'd been involved in the church, and not just in a cursory manner. At 12 I was a Sunday school teacher, I was in women's groups and was a Vacation Bible School leader and on and on. My husband was a pastor and the church was my lifeblood. But still, God had never tapped *me* on the shoulder and said, "Go home, Linotte, it is where you are needed." In fact, He'd never made enquiries of any sort about me staying or going. When He spoke to me, and he often did, it was not about Haiti and certainly not about Carries.

But it was funny that I would head back to Miami and within weeks I'd be feeling sickly again, and more doctors would be seen and time would pass and I wouldn't get well until I would return to Haiti and once there, within days, my ailments would cease.

"God is telling you to return home" Jean Claude would chide again and again, but I didn't want to believe. I had my life and children in Miami and wasn't going to return permanently to the God-forsaken piece of land unless God himself dragged me across the ocean behind a boat.

"Let's go home," my husband would say when I'd be in the midst of one of my spells while back in Florida.

"We *are* home."

"No, to *Haiti*," Jean Claude would say. "I think we need to go back home."

But I would not make such an important decision quickly or lightly.

Upon looking back from a perspective of years, I know there was something lacking in my life that was bundled up inside and seeking a way to escape. Maybe God had been trying to tell me but I hadn't obeyed or understood. But there was a pull in my gut and a twinge in my brain that could not be mistaken, and it was telling me to do something with my life that was more than I'd been doing. It was there in my head rolling around and nipping at me like an annoying little mosquito that keeps flying in your face, and I could feel it, but I didn't know what to do.

Not until the mud came.

FIVE
The Earth Moved

Standing as a mute sentry above Carries, Mount Nan Palmis is neither imposing nor grand. It is not photogenic except as a heavy backdrop for the village beneath. From below it appears to be little more than a large rock covered with scraggly vegetation of russet and olive hues. Up close, its rocky terrain is loose under the foot and to wheedle something of value from its harsh face is next to impossible, though many have tried with little success.

The village snakes its way up the mountain in many trails that were carved out from the natural formation of the ground and not by the plans of men. What can be considered the village darts in and out of the valleys and crags with the density thinning the higher one gets. Those who live up higher tend to be even poorer than those in the lowlands.

Low hanging clouds sometimes obscure the mountain's crest but most often the landscape is baked hard by a relentless sun that offers little relief. When the rains come, and they do twice a year during the rainy seasons, gullies form from Nan Palmise's cracks and crevices and combine with others so the water runs quickly and unimpeded.

No one would have planned a village to be placed where it is, instead the village grew up and around the worst of the landscape and people have tried to live with the setting as best one can.

The day of the rain and mud was by no means extraordinary. As it often does, the rain had been falling for hours and hours, but it was not the worst deluge I, or the people of Carries, had ever witnessed. The rains often fell hard and it rarely caused a large problem and was most often a simple inconvenience. People sat in their homes and waited out the storm or trudged through the rain-swept dirt roads to get to where they needed to be. There certainly was no use in complaining because that wouldn't stop the rains, and so the skies were watched for a break in the clouds and soon enough, life and ordinary routines could continue. Oh, maybe some of the villagers prayed to God, and maybe some summoned a darker spirit, but the rains eventually stopped, and the clouds left, and the sun came out and life was normal in Carries.

It was particularly hot and steamy that day, but if that had been the worst of the afternoon no one would have complained too loudly. It was often steamily hot after the rains and though unbearable to outsiders, it was an unavoidable fact to the residents of Carries who had no recourse but to stay and sweat it out. For them, there was neither escape nor respite.

Late in the afternoon, near to dusk when there was

still light but the day would soon be turning to night, high up on the mountain the earth started to move on a sliver of land perhaps fifty yards wide. In that late afternoon, death came knocking on the doors of Carries.

Ravaged by the rains, a splinter of the mountain sought escape from that which had held it in captivity since the beginning of time. Cleaved from its foundation and broken free with no obstacle to keep it from rolling downhill, it quickly gathered speed and took everything in its path as its plaything. Breaking free of its tenuous hold on the land the mudslide's limbs stretched wide as it tumbled and ground unchecked as it grasped for victims.

I have been told that the mudslide would have moved quicker than anyone might have expected and before one was able to think about what was happening, it would have been upon them. In just a few quick moments, that hot day would have become a race against death and it is often Mother Nature who has the upper hand in such contests.

The path of the mudslide would have been cleared like a machete through weeds and what had been was soon replaced by a roiling mass. The sound was variously described as a wet and living roar, the rumble of a locomotive or the gnashing of teeth and all that amidst the screams of those who attempted to escape its path and those who couldn't. The lucky ones were passed by and those spared became voyeurs off to the side watching a wreck in progress.

The rolling terrain of mud and debris left in its wake a four foot high form of gelatinous goo and a trail of destruction. Tens of dozens of homes, maybe as many as two hundred, were flattened or rendered uninhabitable beneath four feet of thick mud. Walls were knocked down, windows invited the mud in and doors couldn't hold back the sludge. The whole path of destruction was strewn with rocks of every size, from as small as one's finger to as big as a small car. Whole lifetimes of accumulation had been taken away in a few seconds and that might sound trite until one realizes how little the people of the village accumulate, perhaps just some kitchen materials, a few pieces of clothing and some rudimentary furniture, and all of it owned with pride and all but unobtainable again. When each day is a struggle even under the best circumstances, to have been thrown a punch such as what the mud had brought was, quite simply, a matter of survival. Gone was whatever food the victims had in storage, including their goats and chickens and for many, the prospect of starving to death was a stark reality. Even amongst those who walked away unharmed and seemingly unscathed there was the prospect of death. The villagers were too poor to care for those other than their own, and even that was often impossible. In Carries, death could rear its head in a hundred different ways even without mudslides.

But the mudslide *had* brought death to the slope of

Nanpalmise. Those poor unlucky souls who couldn't escape from the grasp were swept up and taken. Ten or fifteen people, perhaps, or twenty-five, or maybe more because no one could ever know for sure about such things in Haiti where no one is ever truly accounted for. Some of the bodies might still be buried in that place, now long buried beneath the terrain and a silent part of the landscape, their graves became where they happened to fall or where the mud had taken them.

That late afternoon people cried for what had happened. They cried for their homes that no longer were and for their loved ones who'd gone from living, to having lived.

SIX
In the Beginning

It was September 2009 when the mudslide came and I was living behind the gates at Ocean View and virtually unaware of what was happening in the village just across the two lane highway. I came and went with blinders on and didn't want to know what was happening not forty feet from where my property ended. If I ventured to the village, it was only to attend the Baptist church that was set back from the highway only a few dozen yards, so I didn't have to see all that lay beyond, but I'd only done so a handful of times. I must have envisioned what was down the goat paths and rocky ways that could be seen from the highway, and I must have given thought to the people that lived up on the hillside, but I'd never given them any great concern and I certainly had never tried to learn more. What would be the purpose of *that*? I was content to come and go and never worried about those things I couldn't see.

On the day of the rains I knew something had happened up on the hill because you could not keep from hearing it, and there at the resort one had to wonder if what we heard was the mudslide, or our hearts, or even a shout from God. It was apparent that something of importance had taken place, but what it was I didn't know until a short time after, and neither I, nor the village, would ever be the same again.

The gate at Ocean View is guarded by an armed guard. He wears a pistol on his hip by day and carries a shotgun by night. We have never had a problem but one can never be too careful in Haiti where turmoil is a national sport and, for a time, kidnappings were common and even touched my family when my younger brother was snatched off the street and held for four days until a ransom was paid.

When the security guard at the front gate came to my room and said, "There are many people out front screaming for help" I looked at him and said, "Help? From what?" because I had no conception of what was happening across the road, but whatever it was had come and found me, and in retrospect, I know that it was *God* who had found me. For too long of a time He'd been tapping me on the shoulder to get my attention and I'd given Him scant attention at all even as I went to church and did all those simple things that makes us believe we're being obedient, and so He tried a new tactic — instead to tapping me on the shoulder He broke out a hammer.

Of course, I went to see what the clamor was all about, and as I crossed the property I saw a lot of mud and water running throughout, and the gate seemed to be acting as a dam. I could hear something taking place outside and didn't hesitate to have the gate opened. Out on the highway and up against the outside wall of the resort there was a sea of oozing mud that seemed alive as it was cast and sloshed about. And though one could be transfixed with the mud because it seemed to have *life* and it seemed unnatural to see it in that light, it was the people who were most compelling as they appeared stunned and confused at what had happened. They held their children close to their chests and had sunken eyes of people who appeared lost. And without any thought I invited those who were appealing for help or relief to come in to Ocean View because Jesus would not have hidden himself behind a gate, so how could *I*.

Because I thought the men could find a way on their own, I took all the women and children in, and opening the gate that day was the start of the Mission of Grace. And as people came pouring through the gate I looked into the faces of the children and they were the first of the Children of Grace.

There were 89 in total who spent the night as God's guests, and I found every available sheet, mattress and towel to make them comfortable. And as I did my best to get them through the first hours of turmoil and tragedy, I looked into their faces and saw that they were scared and tired from what had happened, and apprehensive for what lay ahead. I stayed up until very late that night, looking over my flock and a spirit was found in me that had been clamoring to get out for a long time. Although I have five children of my own, in its own special way, that night I felt like a mother to all 89 of those women and children, regardless of their ages. A motherly instinct is often talked about and if such a thing really exists, then it kicked in for me that night. I felt the pains, I wished them on myself, and I cried for an unknown future, and all this for people I didn't even know, but I knew that *God* had bestowed them on me and that they were in my charge.

In the morning, even before my little clan had awoken from a night of slumber, I knew they'd have to be fed and I went to the cupboards to find something, *anything*, that would be able to fill the stomachs of so many. After searching about, what I found in abundance was spaghetti. I can't even imagine why we had so much spaghetti, but there it was and I know it was a blessing from God.

With my cook and an assistant, we fired up the burners and boiled the water and made pot after pot of spaghetti, and we had to feed the people in shifts. It took a couple of hours before everyone had been fed, but they were, by the grace of God, and that was the first meal ever served by the Mission of Grace. And it was also just about the happiest day of my life. I knew in my mind there would be a time before that day, and a time after. Even as I was living in that moment I knew that something had been radically changed in my life. Often times it takes many years of perspective to understand fully what has happened, but I knew right then and there that a new phase of my life had begun. And upon reflection, to look back at what has been and what has been done, it is amazing what God has allowed to take place in a short period of time since the spaghetti.

I am always quick to tell the spaghetti story, as a reminder to me and as a reminder to others that from humble beginnings great things can come. I've spoken about that night and morning dozens of times at churches, to groups, for missionaries or anyone who's willing to listen because it's a lesson in how great is our God.

My story, or testimony, or mission, or ministry, call it *whatever* you want, started that night and morning, and I am just a little person, but I have a very big God, and without Him, nothing would have been possible, and with Him, *all* things are possible.

SEVEN
To the Other Side

After feeding my guests, I got down on my knees and asked God what I should do *then,* and He told me quite clearly to keep the children. Now I am not averse to crazy ideas but even I thought that sounded like a *crazy* idea and I wondered how I'd go about keeping a bunch of children who weren't mine, but I listened to God and obeyed and I sent the women away and I was left with more than 50 children. And I looked at those children and wondered, "What do I do now, God?" and at that *very* moment I realized that God had been knocking at my gate for a very long time and that He'd been preparing me, even back in my childhood days when I taught Sunday school, for the moment at hand. That may sound self-serving but I know it to be true. We are often in training even if we don't know what we're training *for,* but God has His plan and when He's ready to spring a portion of it upon us we need to have the tools to accept the challenge.

I also knew with clarity and direction that my husband had been right and I also knew what I must do. It wasn't like I had a choice because when you have something to do that's been sent by God, it's not a matter of choice, it's *obedience.* I'd already listened to

Him in sending the mothers away, and there He was commanding me again. And again I listened even though I wasn't yet aware of the scope of my task.

And in that moment when I was given direction without blueprints, and vision without precision, I thought of a nearby pastor, Pastor Edmond, who'd sometimes said to me, "Linotte, if you ever want to open a church here in Carries, let me know" and I'd look at him amusingly and reply "Why *would* I?" because up until that very moment I hadn't ever wanted to open up a church and couldn't have thought of a single reason why I'd need to. It had taken the rain, mud, spaghetti and a whole troop of kids living at my resort—and *God*, for me to understand.

And I knew that one day I would build a church in Carries.

Although my family didn't want me to, I crossed the ribbon of highway that had always been as much a wall, to see for myself the devastation wrought on the village the day before by the rains and mud. And my family might have protested my actions but no one tells me what I cannot do. And as I toured the other side of the highway, and saw what *was* with a hazy vision of what *had* been, and saw the ruined houses and ruined lives, I knew that I could not let those people go. Was I so special or so important that I could just walk away as if it wasn't staring me in the face telling me to get involved? Hadn't God commanded me *to* get involved? And in my travels on the hillside that day I saw a group of people trying to retrieve the body of a boy who'd died in the mud, and as I stood there watching that sad scene of life having been played out, and watched them digging and pulling him out of the thick muck, his head was pulled off his shoulders and something like that will shake you to the core and make you question every aspect of your life, especially your belief in a merciful God, and I stood there in tears watching that sad surreal scene and said "God, what is the reason I am here?" and I didn't know if 'here' was at that exact place on a muddy hill, or in Carries, or in Haiti, but *whatever* the right answer was, I knew that I could no longer hide behind the gates, both physical and spiritual. Sometimes you have to fling open the gates and let those things *out* that are holding you back and to let those things *in* that will allow you to succeed. Sometimes it is not easy to open the gates because few people like to explore the unknown, instead we like what's comfortable and safe. No one likes to be out in the storm, we want to be in safe harbor, but in exploration there can be found holiness and godliness if we allow ourselves to accept God's blessings, to be moved by His spirit and to find out what He has in store for us.

To confirm that I was on a path, I called my best friend in Florida, Violet Benoit, who is a pastor's wife, my prayer partner and I trust her judgement above all others save my husband's. "I think I need to help these people. What do you think?" I asked.

Without hesitation, she replied, "I knew God didn't send you to Haiti for no reason" and that was confirmation that I was on the right path.

There is irony in what came a couple of days after the mudslide, when a white guy that I remember only as 'Rodney' stopped by to see me on his way to Port-au-Prince. I don't know how he found me but when he did he asked, "What are you doing with all these children?" and I told him the story about the mudslide and God commanding me to take the children in.

"What do you *need*?" he then asked, and it might sound sort of silly, but I told him, "I need spoons" because I didn't have enough silverware and we had to feed the children in shifts. Rodney had been expecting me to ask for much more, and he went on his way and amazingly, the next morning he came back with 100 pounds of rice, hundreds of bags of beans and a lot of clothes, and I have to smile when I remember the blessing we received at that early moment when the mission was just hatching. And, of course, he brought spoons, *hundreds* of them. Rodney was sent by God, and those were the first donations to the Mission of Grace.

I kept the children at the resort for two weeks after the mudslide and gradually many went home because school was starting up again and their families could provide for them. The numbers slowly dropped down until there were just five children left and somehow I knew they were mine, but I didn't see what I was doing as an orphanage. Although I already knew the name, that it was Children of Grace, it wasn't *really* an orphanage because the kids had a Father in God, and they had a Mama in me, and a Papa in my husband. I don't know how I knew that those five would be mine forever and always, only that I *did* know. And all these years later, those five are still with me today, thriving in the Children of Grace:

Ginette: Her mother died of AIDS and her father had a new lady who had four children of her own and she didn't want Ginette around so she was being given away, and I gladly took her.

Josette: Her father was an older man and she was extremely sick with white fungus spots on her head among other maladies, and I took her so she would get treatment. A few months later she was still sick and her father came back for her and when I steadfastly refused he put a voodoo spell on her. "Go away!" I yelled at him. "I'm not giving her back—you'll take her to the voodoo doctor and she'll die" and so she stayed with me.

Karline: She was very sick with various medical conditions. Her eyelids had puss draining from them, she was malnourished and she was covered in sores that we thought were caused by AIDS. When I found her out on the street I simply said to those nearby, "Tell her mom I'm taking her" and that's what I did. I never knew much about her parents except that they were very poor. She is sometimes loud and demonstrative, and has a mean streak that is quite annoying, but if she gets to know you a bit, she is funny and loving and has a great future in store. And she is mine.

Jameson: Jameson's mother was just 17 years-old and really just a child herself when her son was born. When he would cry, as all newborn infants will, she would hit him viciously and of course that did little good in keeping him quiet and only exasperated her frustrations. When he came to us, it was extremely sad because he was very mean and though his demeanor has been improved over time, he still carries the deep and dark emotional scars of his early childhood.

Samantha: Her mother had three or four other children in their poor home high up in the mountains and she was overwhelmed, distraught and seemed to be on the verge of a breakdown because her husband had died and she could not support the family alone. Her mother begged me to keep Samantha and so I did.

EIGHT
Poor, Poor Masaline

After the mudslide I was drawn to cross the road. I said to myself, "Would Jesus lock himself behind a gate?" Several years ago the phrase "What would Jesus do?" (WWJD) was all the rage in the Christian community, and it's a pretty good question to ask of those who are trying to live lives like Jesus taught us to live. And in essence, I was asking that very question: What would Jesus do? and the answer was obvious, that He would not hide behind a gate and as such, neither could I.

Still, to cross the road was forbidding because across the road was not of my world, but as I ventured over the blacktop to the other side, and talked to the people, and shed tears with them, and saw the abject poverty in which they lived, how could I just turn my head and pretend *not* to see any longer? I could not, not when I *had* seen.

And so I ventured out, and was seen, and became known. The villagers called me 'Madam Jean' or simply 'Mama.' They knew where I could be found and that I could help with whatever they might need. And as I walked along the dusty and rocky paths that are the roads of Carries, the vision of what it *could* be was coming to me at a quickened pace. I already knew that it would be changed for the better because that had been ordained to me by God, but to what extent was only known *to* God, but in His infinite wisdom, and in His own timing, He was revealing things to me.

Many people up on the hill were skeptical that a woman such as me would climb that mountain because none ever had before, except an occasional missionary, perhaps. But here *was* a woman slogging through the dirt, sitting at people's tables and sharing in their lives. Never had such a thing been done, at least not in Carries, perhaps not in all of Haiti!

And even then, very early on, they would come up to me and call me as I walked the dusty roads, and they would hold my hand. And I would touch them and tell them that they're loved by me and by God, and I'd bring them food and I would pray for them. And amazingly, just my presence would give them encouragement and made them feel as if they weren't just forgotten souls of society.

Within a week of the mudslide, while I still had more than two dozen children living at the resort, someone came down and knocked on the gate to speak to me and when I came out I was told there was a pregnant woman up on the mountain who'd been in labour for 24 hours. I got my longtime employee, Jolem, to take me up the mountain to the shanty in which the young woman lay.

It amazes me the conditions in which some people live. I shouldn't be taken aback at what I sometimes see, but I often am nonetheless. It seems to me that everyone should have a minimal standard to live by, and yet, particularly in Haiti, many do not, or perhaps it's that our standard is so low it would be difficult to miss the mark. Perhaps my baseline of what is acceptable and what is not, is higher, and I want better for *all* people. Haiti has failed countless peoples in its long history and the poorest of the poor are those most often failed.[1]

To call the place I was taken to a "house" would be a lie and to call it a "shanty" would be giving it more than it was due. It was where people lived and that will have to suffice because it was no better or worse than a hundred others in the community. I will not give the impression that it was anything great while I want the reader to understand that it was hardly worthy for people to lay their heads at night. If everyone living in that shanty exhaled at the same time the walls might have collapsed right on them.

The poor pregnant woman was very weak and in extreme pain, but she was also prayerful that she would be rescued from what she was enduring. And

---

[1] Haiti's circumstance of being the poorest nation in the Western Hemisphere is well documented. Its Gross Domestic Product per capita is $820, less than one-tenth of the Latin American average. Sixty percent of the population lives below the poverty line and the richest 20 percent accounts for 62 percent of the income. Amazingly, only 500,000 people out of a population of 11 million have permanent employment.

on seeing that young girl, I said to myself, "These people have *nobody*" and I knew then, from that moment on, they would have someone; that they would have *me*, and I don't make myself out to be more than I am, because it's all from God.

It was late in the afternoon when I went down the mountain to arrange transportation to take the woman to the hospital since it was too late to catch a ride on a tap-tap for the short ride up the coast to Saint Marc where a doctor and clinic could be found. But as I was in the process of getting a car and a driver, word came down from the mountain that the young woman had finally delivered the baby, but both the child and she had died.

Her name was Masaline, a beautiful Haitian name for a beautiful Haitian girl who died well before she needed to. At the time of her death, Masaline might have been 22, or 25, no one knew for sure because high up on the mountain education was a rarity and calendars were rarer still. All anyone really knew was that she'd been born, she'd led a difficult life (because everyone in Carries does) and that she'd died.

In some respects, she was the first in the mission, or, at the least the first to have a name attached so her story could be remembered and passed on. In time, people would say, "Remember when?" and her story would be told and there was a time before Masaline and there is a time after, the two apparent only to those who had been witness to both.

Sadly, I cannot recall Masaline's *last* name but she is not forgotten, at least not by those who know her story.

I was heartbroken and crestfallen as I climbed back up the mountain and when I saw the family, and grieved with them as they wailed loudly, not only for their deceased loved one Masaline, and for her child who never even got to see a single day of life, but also in despair for their place in life and because there was no money for a proper burial. And as I came back down the mountain I knew what must be done. So many young women were dying because there was no prenatal care and the unborn were left to God's mercy, but something *could* be done to protect our precious children. It wasn't even something I could debate because it was God speaking to me, and when God speaks it's best to listen. The people up on the mountain had no hospital, but if there *had been*, two lives could have been saved, and that is what I thought as I came down the mountainside that day, and I knew immediately that as sure as I breathe, and as sure as I know that God is real, and as sure as I was that what I was doing was mandated by God, that I would find a way to provide a place for people to go for healthcare. I didn't know exactly what, how, when or where, only that there *would* because I'd somehow make sure it happened. It was as if God had placed the burden on my shoulders to do His bidding.

And that day I was reminded again, that when God approves, he provides, and that all things are possible with Him.

At the time of Masaline's death, the Mission of Grace was already a week old, although it did not have an official name and no one besides me really knew that it had already begun. It would only be later, when there was time to give even a bit of reflection, that it was realized that a mudslide and a particular death were the beginnings of what would prove to be something much larger and ever expanding.

Masaline was not buried in Carries' cemetery, and where she is buried is known only to those family members who might recall under which rocks her body was placed. Like most of the poorest of the poor in Carries, her body was likely taken even further up the mountain and buried privately in a shallow grave.

NINE
The House Began to Shake

Many Haitians believe that God has forgotten them, or at the very least, ignores them, because He has bigger and more pressing problems than to worry about a poor little country like Haiti. Many also think He treats them unfairly, for reasons unknown, when compared to the rest of the world, although He treats them with no more or no less ill will. But still, the mistaken beliefs that God has abandoned Haiti, or looks the other way at its predicament, *seemed* to have been supported by the earthquake that hit the country at 4:53 PM on January 12, 2010.

Haiti has had more than its fair share of woes and catastrophes, both natural and manmade, and that such an event should take place in a country so poor does seem unfair. There can be no accurate accounting of how many died—150,000 seems too low and 500,000 seems too high, but no one would really argue with 300,000, and it's been suggested that everyone in the country personally knew at least one person who perished. Something like 3% of the country's population died and to put that in perspective, if that same 3% was to die in the United States, the total would be more than 9 million people.

On top of the deaths, over 200,000 residences were destroyed along with 30,000 commercial buildings, and the country's infrastructure, always on tenuous footing at best, collapsed completely. More than six years later the country is still trying to get out from under the rubble that the earthquake dropped on Haiti.

It is an unfortunate truth that Haiti was built terribly. The country has no building codes and buildings go up with no real thought given to the fact that one day, under harsh circumstances, they might come down. With no rules, regulations, standards or any thought about safety, when the earthquake hit thousands *did* come tumbling down and in its wake were an untold number of dead.

Because my husband was going to Florida for a few weeks, he was going to spend the night before his flight at our home in Port-au-Prince so he wouldn't have far to travel in the morning. As Jolem was driving us to the city, Jean Claude casually said to us, "Something is going to happen today."

"Like what?" I asked.

My husband shrugged his shoulders and said, "An earthquake, perhaps."

I looked at him like he was nuts in the head. "Have you lost your mind?" I said, and then I turned to Jolem. "Don't listen to him, he must be crazy because he's never even experienced an earthquake."

Jean Claude didn't respond except to say, "I have to say what the Lord told me."

Once we'd settled in at home, Jean Claude decided to go out for a haircut and we had a discussion over where he should go and how he should get there. He wanted to walk down the road to a barbershop and I wanted him to go to a place farther away and to drive. Since it was not my hair being cut, Jean Claude had his way.

He'd only been gone for a short time when the house began to shake and my first thought was that Jesus was returning but I found it curious there were no trumpets (Revelation 11:15 — Then the seventh angel blew his trumpet, and there were loud voices in heaven, saying, 'The kingdom of the world has become the kingdom of our Lord and of his Christ, and he shall reign forever and ever!').

To be honest, I stood there as if rooted to the floor, unsure of what I should do or where I should go. When your world is being upended right in front of your eyes I'd guess there are two ways to react; either you run about and scream frantically or just watch. I was of the second group and it was unnerving but it almost seemed as if I was *incapable* of doing anything. One of my employees came running through the house and saw me just standing in the living room screaming and he picked me up and threw me through an open window.

And though it *seemed* I was in a safer place, it

certainly didn't seem *safe*, so instead of just standing waiting as a witness for a wall to fall on my head and kill me, I decided to be a participant in my escape from harm. If I was going to die, I'd rather die running. I am not a fast runner, but my legs hadn't moved faster in a very long time as I made a mad dash for safer haven.

Outside didn't seem a whole lot better than inside and as the world seemed to be coming to an end I started to pray to Jesus, that if it was that time then He would treat me mercifully, and that if it was my time to go then I was ready for his judgment of me. And I really believed my time *had* come, especially when our hot water heater blew up with a loud BOOM and all of us who were outside started hurrying like ants because explosions added another layer to the chaos, as if anything more was needed.

And it was only then that I realized I was in the middle of an earthquake. It might sound silly, but if you've never experienced one, it made more sense that it was anything *but*.

From our front yard I could see the apartment building next door, in which lived a lot of United Nations workers, and I was more than a little shocked to see a half-dozen of them running naked out of the building as it was swayed back and forth. And it was in the little surreal tableau that I knew things were going to be bad. When a whole apartment building could sway like a palm tree in the breeze, what of the other buildings? And what of the *people*?

When my husband came running up to the house I praised God and he told me that when the quake hit he ran outside the barbershop and watched as hell was being unleashed, and as he stood outside the barbershop watching the calamity unfold, the building directly across the street fell flat in a crumpled heap right before his eyes. Soot and ash created a plume that engulfed all those in its path and nearly turned day into night. And though I hadn't been out on the streets yet, and had yet to witness the calamity as Jean Claude had, I knew that the nightmare was only just beginning.

Out on the streets it was not good and what I saw I do not like to remember or recount and will do so only with a glance. I saw children's bodies cut up and left out in the open. I saw a girl with a blue ribbon in her hair but her body had been cut in half. I saw bodies under sheets lined up like cords of wood. And *everywhere* you turned there were snapshots like those; of destruction, death and devastation. It could not be escaped from. The only way to keep from seeing was to close your eyes, but in such a situation one cannot go blind, it must be seen as if it's a part of life. I will be haunted by the deaths, and the manners in which death came, for the rest of my life.

Every member of my family went out to see what we could do. We made a little tent city at the apartment complex my brother owns, and at his home's compound we gave the water from his cistern to hundreds of people. People cried at our gate because we gave them a cookie and there were tears everywhere you turned, but they were muffled and almost silent. People were in shock and they didn't know what to say.

The first night was the most bizarre of my life. As the city around us wracked and writhed with aftershocks, as the screams of a million crying people covered the city, as the groans of voices and twisted metal and stone blanketed the landscape, it was as if we were in the depth of misery and hell. If Dante's *Inferno* was a true place on earth, then it would have been in Port-au-Prince that first night after the earthquake.

In the morning we made spaghetti and when we ran out of plates we put food on napkins. One old man, dirty and bent, pulled out a nasty and filthy handkerchief from his pocket and we put spaghetti on that and he was so thankful because he hadn't eaten in over 24 hours. He said to me, "Momma, thank you. I now have the strength to go on to find my son" and I pray that his son survived and that the two were reunited. There must have been a hundred-thousand stories like that, and not all of them would have had happy endings. As the numbers rolled in of the dead and injured, the magnitude was nearly overwhelming.

We did what we could, although even in hindsight it seems underwhelming. In my brother's compound we opened up the gates to 50-60 people and we fed them and kept them safe as the aftershocks hit. We kept them for six days and amidst the carnage I would pray to God, "What can I do?" and we tried to carry the burden of at least a few people, but there were *millions* affected.

And even in the first few hours, help started to pour in to Haiti, first from the Dominican Republic and then from around the world. Countries set aside their differences to help out a poor little country that most people couldn't even find on a map.

TEN
Strangers

With assistance and aid pouring into Haiti from all over the world, I decided to leave the capital for Ocean View and to open our gates to those who were helping the cause. At the resort I felt I could be most effective and that with thousands of aid workers coming in from all around the globe, they'd need a place to stay or a place to spend an afternoon relaxing every once in a while.

It was eerie to leave Port-au-Prince and the destruction there and to see caravans of open trucks taking tangled bodies to be buried in mass graves not ten miles outside the city in the village of Titiyen. It is not the sort of vision one ever expects to see in a lifetime and there it was in front of us and sometimes even today it haunts my dreams.

It was a relief to travel up the coast and away from the ruins of not only the structures, but people's lives. When I got to Carries I ran into a woman who owns the large property near to ours and she said to me, "Lynn, let's go, we're getting out of here" but I couldn't leave, not when people were coming in from all four corners of the globe to help. It would have been easy to get a flight out of the country, but I would have felt like a coward if I left, and so I stayed.

Once I was sure about the decision to stay I got down on my knees and asked God what I could do, and I went to bed with no assured answer.

At six the next morning our security guard came and woke me up to tell me that there was a group of people at the gate. "What do they want with me?" I asked, but I didn't get an acceptable answer so I got dressed to find out.

The man waiting for me at the gate was a white guy who was heading to Port-au-Prince from the Dominican Republic with a group of people and was going to need a place to sleep after they unloaded their truck. We made arrangements and when he returned later that night we stayed up late talking of the earthquake and what we'd seen. He told me he was coming back in a few days and when he did he brought 5,000 sandwiches with him, and good ones, too, and what seemed like a million bottles of water. "What am I supposed to do with this?" I asked, and though he didn't have an answer, he imagined I'd be able to find a way to distribute them, and I did. I had them taken to the town of Delma, just aside of the capital that had been completely devastated, and had them distributed to tent cities. And he kept dropping off food at Ocean View for the next three months, and I kept finding needy people for it to be delivered to.

We had contingents from the United Nations who showed up with some regularity including one group of twenty headed by a guy who couldn't pay, but asked if he could give me anything, but I couldn't think of anything in particular. "I have radios," he told me, and a couple of days later he delivered 300 solar radios that we distributed to the village. He also brought hundreds of kits of food and medicines that we could distribute as needed to the people of Carries. And then his commander came and gave me stuff and he was an early bridge to the Mission of Grace.

One of the men from a church in New Jersey, Pastor Soaries, brought a group to eat and go swimming at the resort. He sat down with me at length and I told him about the village and what had taken place over the preceding months, and then I took him up the hill to show him around. At one point we stopped and he told me, "Linotte, God is going to bless this ground" and he prayed and dedicated the ground where our first orphanage would rise, not that I knew an orphanage *would* rise. And as we were walking back to Ocean View the pastor asked what I was going to do for Easter. "Do?" I asked.

"You should have a big Easter dinner," he said and then pulled $600 out of his pocket to pay for a community dinner. In light with what would come later, I know the pastor was heavenly sent because life would have been much different without that dinner.[1]

A few weeks later I was in Florida sharing at my

---

[1] Easter dinners are now a tradition as we've fed the community every Easter Sunday since that first one.

church about all that had been going on in Haiti, and afterwards, one of the active brothers, Brother Daniel, said to me, "Who knew you were a missionary?" and I kind of laughed it off, but he was adamant that I was doing missionary work and that I needed to do more and that the congregation needed to support me. And in one of those fortuitous meetings one sometimes has, Daniel said he had a friend in New York City who wanted to help the Haitian cause but needed a connection. "I'm going to have him call you," he told me, and by 3:00 o'clock that afternoon I'd heard from Daniel's friend, Dr. Lesly Honore, who wanted to have a conference call with me and some other doctors. By 4:00 o'clock we'd all talked and the doctors had scheduled a visit to Carries two weeks later to put on a clinic.

The team arrived as scheduled and in the middle of the clinic one of the doctors, Emmanuel St. Louis, pulled me aside and said, "Linotte, you a have a lot of sick people here."

"Of course, we are poor," I told him.

He crossed his arms and shook his head and said, "I want to help" and we talked for a long time and I know that Doctor St. Louis was one of the angels sent from heaven although the physical fruits of that conversation would not be seen for nearly two years.

ELEVEN
A Desperate Struggle

I take comfort that an important part of my life, and this story, took place on Easter Sunday, April 4, 2010, when we opened up the gates of Ocean View and fed over 600 people as Pastor Soaries had wanted. We went all out and had Creole chicken and rice with cake and soda and when everyone had eaten there was music and dancing and people were happy like I've never seen in the village.

It was while people waited in line to get their food that I had one of those moments that are only too rare in life. It was a moment that very easily might not have happened and it was years before I really understood its implication and importance, and perhaps I still don't understand fully.

The line wound its way across the property and I was taking the older people from the back and bringing them to the front, and as I was doing so I saw a woman with a child in each of her arms and two more holding onto her legs. The children were black as oil, skinny as skeletons and filthy dirty, as if they'd rolled around in the dirt before coming down the mountain to eat. Once I set eyes on the five doleful souls I brought them to the front of the line and got someone to help get their food.

I learned the woman's name was Marie-Angé and when I saw her putting food in the mouths of the two boys she was holding in her arms I stopped her and said, "You can't give those babies whole food, they'll choke," but Marie-Angé looked at me with a funny sort of glare and said, "They're not babies, they're almost eleven months old."

The woman must have been crazy or was trying to make a joke, so I stepped in closer to get a better look and after examining the two I said, "No, they're *babies*," but she insisted they weren't babies at all.

The children were so small that I found it un-believable that they weren't just infants, but then it hit me that they were malnourished, and it was the first time I realized that children were dying of starvation in Haiti. And I watched that little family eat, and it was almost with embarrassment that the two older children put food to their mouths, as if having full bellies was a crime or a sin.

For the rest of the day I couldn't get that little family out of my mind and as the afternoon wore on I just wanted the event to end and to usher everyone out because there was something I had to do. I don't know what it was that made me hurry to finish, but when I have something lodged in my brain I have to act on it or it will gnaw annoyingly like a persistent mosquito.

After we finished serving food to all the people I found someone from the village and said, "Take me to Marie-Angé's home" because I wanted to see where she lived. There is no time like the present to take action and I don't know what sort of action I was to take, but I wasn't going to sit around and wait for a revelation to come to me, I was going to take my revelation to her.

I was taken far up the mountain to a pitiable house that gave me pause even before I stepped onto the property. It was a house in name only and was made of sticks with two pieces of sagging tin and some patchwork cardboard and little else for a roof. If a good wind came the whole thing would have blown off and floated down the mountain. The outside was plenty bad, but the inside was simply misery. It was so hot that the tin was dripping sweat and I found the twin boys, Kichlo and Kichnider, asleep on a dirty sheet atop a little bed made from four bricks with wood slats. The other two children were crying and I stood amazed that people could be living so insufficiently and in such poverty. I looked around and saw little of what makes a house a home. Whatever clothes I could see were really nothing more than rags; there was a gallon bucket with sea salt inside and another bucket for cinders to cook with, but I didn't see anything *to* cook. There was not a single piece of food inside the hovel. In a corner was a bucket of dirty and brackish water and I didn't have the heart to ask if that's what they drank from because I didn't want to hear the answer if it was.

What I supposed was a bed was tucked into the corner and although I couldn't be sure of its use, it looked like a place where people might lie and sleep, but it wasn't really a bed as much as a contraption of dirty sheets atop some sticks so it might pass for the worst sort and most uncomfortable bed possible.

And as I eyed that sad and woeful place, I picked up the smallest baby in my arms and Marie-Angé shook her head slightly and said to me, "I wish he would just die and be out of his misery" and I was shocked that a mother would say such a thing, but in a sad way, I also understood. In her situation she'd done all she could for that child, and it was time to worry about those who had a chance to survive and not have to expend the energy on a child who did not. I imagine that some might find such a sentiment sinful, but in a Third World country, where death lingers nearby and often awaits at one's threshold, and where life, liberty and the pursuit of happiness are foreign concepts, such talk and beliefs are just facts of life. No one will ever know the true number of deaths that takes place up in the hills where nothing has ever been recorded. Death happens with a frequency that few can fathom.

And in that squalor of five living souls, who were "living" as bleak a life as could be possible, I started crying and I looked down at that child in my arms, and he couldn't have weighed more than seven pounds despite being nearly eleven months old, and I stepped outside because inside was hot, dirty and I was feeling claustrophobic or sickly in the presence of man's inequity and inequality. Not that I blamed Marie-

Angé, but I needed to collect myself and to breathe fresh air. And as I looked at the ocean far off in the distance, and as I held that boy, Kichlo, who was as good as dead even as he breathed shallowly in my arms, I prayed a prayer — "Dear God," I said, "today is Easter, the day of resurrection, you raised Lazarus and yourself, and what I hold is a dead baby, but if this baby lives, I know you approve of what I'm doing — that you give approval to the ministry." And then I prayed something that wasn't my own but were words divinely placed on my lips and tongue, perhaps as a reminder of God's greatness, or as a reminder that prayers are often answered, or maybe just so that I will never forget that the whole ministry is about God and not me, or anyone else. That day I also prayed, "And I know that you have someone to help me."

"Let me take this child" I said to Marie-Angé when I went back inside because at the very least I'd have more resources to keep the child alive, not that I thought there was *any* chance of that happening whatsoever. He was as dead as any child who was still breathing. There wasn't even much thought given, or questioning if it was the right thing for her to do, and there appeared to be no moral dilemma. And though I know she loved that child, and would have loved to have kept him with her, her love was so deep that she gave him up so that the life she brought into the world could continue to keep living. It was the only way. If she was to hold onto him she would have been burying him in a shallow grave or under a rock in a day or two, or perhaps a week, but it was going to happen and it was going to happen soon. She knew that, and I knew that, but the only one who didn't know that was *God*.

Marie-Angé let me take her son because he would no longer be a burden to her and it would only be through grace if he was to somehow survive, but he would not, and both Marie-Angé and I were quite certain of that, not that I wouldn't try, and not that Marie-Angé hadn't tried. It was just a fact that some lived and some did not. Some died and we had to go on with our lives even while in mourning.[1]

It's sad that I didn't know people were starving in my own backyard. How blind was I, or naïve was I, to not know such a thing took place in Haiti where calamity of every sort was commonplace. And as I looked about and saw all the miseries that were burdened on my country, and even as the bodies in Port-au-Prince were still being taken to mass graves, I wondered if the job of transforming Haiti, or converting it, was like trying to fill the ocean by tossing in a single rock at a time—an impossible task.

But at that time I wasn't overly concerned with

---

[1] The twin boys were named Kichlo and Kichnider, but after they were given to me, first one and then later the other, their names were changed to Josiah and Joshua because in Creole, the name "Kichlo" literally means "darkness" and we didn't want him saddled with a name with such a negative connotation.

transforming Haiti or even Carries, that would come later, what I was concerned with was how to keep a starving and sick baby alive, and so I turned to about the only person I knew who might give me some clues. All I wanted was to give Josiah a fighting chance. I knew he'd fought a good battle, and he *was* a battler because by all intents and purposes he should have been dead already. With such a low weight at such an age, only one out of a hundred would have survived as long as he had. Perhaps only one in a *thousand*.

I called Dr. St. Louis in New York and explained to him about the baby and how sick he was and asked for any advice that would keep him alive. And the doctor and his sister, Yolaine, a pediatrician, told me what to do and I followed their instructions and I prayed over that child and I had others come in and pray for him, and we never left him alone because at the least we wanted him to know he was loved. If he died, he would go with knowing just that one thing.

And Josiah fought and we fought with him. He struggled and held on until Dr. St. Louis came back to Carries to teach another clinic, and he brought medicines with him that would help keep Josiah alive, and it was on that trip when the doctor said to me, "Linotte, you have to do something" and I told him I wanted to build a hospital and he thought that was too big of an undertaking for a place like Carries at that time. "You need a clinic" he said, and I'd never even thought about a *physical* clinic because it had been lodged in my mind that a *hospital* was needed and having limited medical knowledge I wasn't a hundred percent sure of what a clinic was or could provide, but the doctor educated me and the idea of a clinic was born.

TWELVE
The Little House

I can be persuasive if I want to be. I don't know if people are afraid of me, hate me, or love me, or a combination of all three, but I often get my way — but not always.

I couldn't keep even a small troupe of children at Ocean View indefinitely, it was a business after all and to have children running around and interrupting paying guests wouldn't have been right. I crossed the road and looked for a place for the children to go, not that they wouldn't still be mine because they would, especially those first five, but I needed a place in the community. Jolem has been part of Carries for a long time and with a quiet demeanor he gets things done. He showed me around the village and we went into a few houses before he showed me a small house that was nearly perfect for what I envisioned.

"How much?" I asked the owner, who gave me a number to rent the place. "No, to *buy*?" I asked, but he crossed his arms and shook his head defiantly. And it went back and forth like that for an hour and I didn't get my way and we've been renting the property ever since, and I still try to buy it whenever I have the chance, but the owner is as obstinate as I am.

To turn a little house into a little orphanage didn't take much. We painted the inside and added a toilet out back and cleaned up the yard and that was about it. We hired some nannies and though they initially cooked in the open air beside the building, in time we built a large kitchen aside the house with a porch that has turned into a meeting place where people play dominoes and visit.

In an odd way, it was a sad day when the kids left Ocean View for their new home, but it was also a great day in that a vision became focused. There was a *place* in the village for the vision to grow from and it was our first root to let people know that we were staying.

We as a people tend to celebrate firsts; our first words, steps, day of school, dates, cars and on and on are moments in time that are commemorated, and so too do we as this community commemorate that first little house for what it was and what it has continued to be, a refuge for those who have less than most but have a future when there was none for them before.

THIRTEEN
A Gift From Far North

Kim O'Dwyer's story is worthy of its own book, or a movie, perhaps. She comes from a place in Canada, Dawson Creek, where winter temperatures often drop down to -30° below zero and snow covers the ground for five months out of the year. Of course, in all of recorded history, not one single snowflake has ever fallen on Haiti.

On the day of Haiti's earthquake Miss Kim was in Canada watching news reports of the devastation and asked, "Where's Haiti?" She certainly was not alone and it's probable that *most* people have no idea where Haiti is located.

Kim felt convicted to come to Haiti to help with the earthquake crisis, not for a week or ten days, but for a few months, and when she asked for the time off from her job it was given to her, although she would have quit if need be. Through some of her father's connections[1], a week later she was at the Dominican Republic border and was being taken in a bus to an orphanage in Port-au-Prince. Soon she was living on

---

[1] At that time, Rick O'Dwyer was the Director of Operations for *Gleanings For The Hungry* in California, an important ingredient in the making of the Mission of Grace.

the grounds of the Port-au-Prince police station and doing relief work in a medical tent on the station's roof. Even amidst the carnage and horror of the earthquake's aftermath she'd fallen in love with the country, or at least its people, although she had no personal connection to the land *or* the people.

In March, just two months after the earthquake, the capital was still a chaotic mess and though she didn't want to leave, Kim went home, but not to return to her life in Canada, but to shut down all she had there so she could return to Haiti.

In June she returned to work with a woman who was planning to start a little orphanage and it was in that capacity that we met and came to realize our views and visions were similar, although we had no plan to actually work together. In truth, the manner in which Miss Kim came to me was convoluted and something neither she nor I like to remember or talk about. Suffice it to say, she got involved with people who were not all they professed to be. However, one of the important aspects of our early relationship was that she took Josiah to their orphanage because they were better able to serve him than I was, and it was on taking him that Miss Kim's call for Haiti hit her fully and she committed herself to the country. "I saw the potential for the country," she's said. "Early on I wondered how can I help the future of Haiti and I'm still looking for an answer to that question."

Miss Kim became part of a little orphanage that was

starting up in the southern mountains of Haiti in the village of Plaisance, where I was born and where my mother still lives, although one has nothing to do with the other. The woman she'd partnered with in that venture stayed for only a few weeks before heading to Florida for a month leaving Miss Kim alone with five children, one of whom was Josiah who'd become sick and was once again struggling to stay alive. Night after night Kim slept with him on her chest and she believes to this day that he did not survive because of anything she did for him, but only because it was God's will to keep him breathing. "It wasn't about me or the medicines, it was all about God" she's told innumerable audiences. She also knows that during those months in Plaisance, she and Josiah became committed to each other's lives, that it was a blessing and ordination from God. As she felt his little urchin of a heart breathing on her own chest, the two almost beating as one, she wondered how she could ever let him go, and she prayed to God so he wouldn't go, that he would live *and* that the bond they'd forged would be for eternity.

It was a struggle, though, in Plaisance, with not knowing the language, of being alone and mothering five children, one of whom was on the verge of dying every day, and the cultural differences were all cultivating a despondence and despair. Her psyche was often held intact by a thin string and a good verse. Her father recalls that she would call home to Canada each night and had he known where she was, he would have gone and gotten her and brought her home. "It's so hard" she'd say over and over, but she also told her father that she wouldn't have stayed if God hadn't *called* her to Haiti in the first place, and then He'd called her to stay, and in that belief she was right where she was supposed to be.

Rick O'Dwyer isn't surprised that she did stay despite his fatherly worries, or that she's thrived in her mission. Kim's father is a barrel-chested man whose voice commands his presence and belies his emotions when speaking of his daughter, and the woman she's become; "Growing up was hard for Kim. She was a lot like her mom—strong willed and bullheaded, but despite her struggles, she's prevailed because she's driven and determined." And although a man of few words, he cut to the heart of his daughter by once saying, "She's always been caring and wanted to give back."

I cannot know the mysteries of why people have a heart for one thing and not another, and I will not read into Miss Kim's to try to understand the nuances of how her heart works, all I know, and all I can say is this; she heard God's voice and came, and she loves Haiti and the Haitian people. Why else would she have stayed for these six years when it would have been easy to leave on numerous occasions? Why else would she have stayed in the face of degradation, deprivation and apathy? No one would have faulted her for leaving.

No one would have called her a failure for heading home again, until that day when she knew she *was* home on a sunbaked landscape that was as foreign as the moon, where she didn't know the language and was often looked at as just a *blan*[1] with no respect given

I am reluctant to do so, but to describe Miss Kim in a fitting manner I would say this: she is free with her smiles but they do not come cheaply and seem to be given at a cost, as if she only has so many in her reservoir and they need to be rationed.

She has the square jaw of her father and the intriguing eyes of someone who is looking far down the road or far into the future.

She walks with the confidence and countenance of a Canadian, a feature borne of stoutness and grace.

There is a twinkle in her eye that is rarely shown but when it is, it is well worth the price of admission, but I do not like to be on the receiving end of one of her icy glares.

What she seeks, she finds; what she wants, she will get and those she loves are very blessed to feel that love.

In Plaisance, Kim spent a hellacious few months with the woman she'd partnered with, and then in Saint Marc, just up the coast from Carries, where they'd

---

[1] *blan* = white, and is a name, sometimes used derisively, for Caucasian people.

moved the orphanage, and the two became testy with one another over where they were going, what the future would bring and how things were to be done. But even amidst their disagreements, both knew that Josiah needed to be adopted by one or the other because to give him back to his mother would mean certain death. His life still was not assured and was hanging on a filament. He was still in such a bad state that constant care and prayers were the only things keeping him going, and it was Miss Kim who took it upon herself to be the mother to that child, and later to his brother, because she loved them and knew what her purpose in Haiti was. And, she knew what her purpose in *life* was.

Amazingly, because she knew that one day she would get a call from God, and so sure was she that that call would come, and because she'd wanted to be ready when He called, she'd held normal life at bay and had stayed unencumbered. Life, love, ownership and *things* that might keep her from answering God's call quickly and decisively were foregone or put on hold so that she would be ready when the call came, and it *had* come and she'd listened and followed His instruction to go to Haiti, and once there she heeded and had been the faithful servant. Even when it all seemed *insane*, that her time in Haiti was an exploit that no rational person would want to be a part of, when there was no good reason to stay, and especially when she thought she might lose Josiah and the other children, she *still* put trust in God because how could she not when He'd always guided her down the right path?

And after the long nights, the fears and tears, and the dark months, she was finally able to shed the yoke from around her neck and was able to break free from the shackles of people and circumstances that were keeping her from being her best, and with assistance from those who loved her, she was assured that Josiah and Joshua would remain in her care and *hers*, because even then they were a family.[1] And she knew that hers wasn't only a ministry for those two boys, or those few children, but for a whole community. How great is it to break free of one's cocoon and to soar? How great is it to be able to run with abandon and to be one of God's children? It was a new life for Miss Kim, and to have seen her blossom from that to where she is today has been one of my great joys.

And in her freedom she came and asked if she could work for the Mission of Grace. "I've been waiting for this day" I told her, and we hugged and prayed and tears were shed and she was an answer to my prayer.

Up on the mountaintop, with Josiah in my arms, I'd prayed to God not to save that young boy's life but to show love and benevolence over him, but I'd also asked

---

[1] It took *years*, but in 2016 Miss Kim was granted legal custody of the boys and they are now officially Joshua and Josiah O'Dwyer.

for a consecration of the ministry if He desired, and if He so desired, then to send me someone who'd be a voice, but I never thought it would be a woman let alone a white woman from Canada, but Miss Kim is the voice God sent and I am blessed that she was.

People ask me all the time what I think of Miss Kim and how does one reveal love of the heart? The greatest writers in history haven't been able to express love in words and so why should I even try? But I will say this:

She is my Aaron.

She serves me.

She is my guardian angel.

She is loyal to me.

She protects me.

But most importantly, she protects the *vision*.

FOURTEEN
A Very Important Napkin

Miss Kim's arrival to me and to the Mission of Grace coincided with a very important event in my history and in the mission's.

I was reading the Bible one day when there was a knock at the door and I was told there was a man to see me. "Who is he?" I asked, but I was given no real answer. The man was Fritz Meier, who was then a director at *Gleanings for the Hungry* in California and he'd heard about what I was doing in Carries and wanted to see for himself. Fritz is a tall and wiry man with the whisper of a Swiss accent and has sharp eyes that are questioning and wandering. He is difficult to read and as interesting a person as you would ever meet.

After we'd talked for a while he said, "Take me to see the kids," and I took him across the street to the little house and he looked at it and he met the children and finally said to me, "Oh, Miss Lynn, we have to build you an orphanage." And I always knew that God was going to give us a bigger house, I just didn't know how or when or by whom.

Fritz and I went back to Ocean View and sat down at a table and he asked "What would you like in an orphanage?" and I started talking and he grabbed a napkin off the table and started sketching what an orphanage might look like. I told him we would need a wide porch, a dining room and two sides, one for boys and one for girls and on and on. In less than an hour we had the basic plans and when we were satisfied Fritz said, "Let's pray" and we did and he left.

When Fritz returned a few days later the first thing he asked was, "Miss Lynn, do you have land?" and I told him that I'd talked to the mayor of the region and he was willing to get me the land I needed. "I want to bring my Discipleship Training School team here, but I want to break ground on faith" and so we did.

Rick O'Dwyer, Kim's father, ran *Gleanings* at that time and he came to Carries and approved funds for the orphanage, a contractor was hired and he stayed at the ministry for a year and a half, planning, supervising and building. It's amazing how quickly things can come together in Haiti where permits, inspections or even plans aren't needed. *Our* plans were on the back of a napkin, but we had vision for what the job would look like when it was finished, and what its purpose would be far into the future.

And construction moved quickly and we hired our first employee, a nannie named Medina.

Having escaped from chains that were anchoring her to a rock that couldn't be seen, Miss Kim took some time to arrange the rest of her life and joined the Mission of

Grace just as our first orphanage building was being built. She lived at Ocean View with the eight orphans she'd had in Saint Marc, who became ours, and matched the number that my original five had grown into.

On the appointed date Miss Kim left Ocean View with her eight in tow and marched like a junior parade down the highway and across into the village and to the little house where my eight awaited, and those two groups joined into one, the Children of Grace. As one we marched hand in hand, singing songs and carrying all our possessions with us, even our mops, to the new home, and it was a glorious sight for those lucky enough to have seen or taken part.

There are moments in life that you like to look back on because of the fondness they bring. They are our "go to" moments that can lessen the effects of a bad day or they can bring a ray of sunshine to a cloudy day. For me, moving into the new house was one of those days. The Mission of Grace was already a year-old and though we had sixteen children in our charge, we hadn't become part of the community as I'd envisioned. By that original building being built, it meant we were making a commitment, not only to the children, but to the place where they would live.

At the gate we said a prayer and then let the children into their new home and we have never left there and it has only grown.

I often think about those first sixteen, and especially

my first five, and they bring a smile to my face when I see them in the orphanage. I dream of where their futures lie. I trust that God will take care of them just as I trust that God will take care of the mission wherever it may lead us.

There was never really a question that Miss Kim would be director of the orphanage. She was the one I'd prayed for and she was the one God sent to me. Even then, very early in our friendship and relationship, I knew that she was mine and I was hers. We would work together until God called one of us home or away to another place. If that day never happens, it would be fine with me.

Instead of living at Ocean View, Miss Kim encamped in a room at the orphanage. She worked tirelessly with the children and set up a foundation of what the mission would be far into the future. Of course it would be based on Christian values, and it would be filled with love, those were givens, but there had to be a *feel* in what we were building and she was the one who put that in home, the intangible of what a *culture* is to any place.

And it was interesting, that as she marched about the village, not only back and forth to Ocean View, but up to the hills to see people, or down into the valleys to deliver food, this young woman of just thirty, who was working tirelessly for a just cause with little return except for God's glory, was looked at maliciously by many villagers who saw only a black and white issue — she was a *blan* and as such she couldn't, or wouldn't, be trusted. And tirelessly I kept telling them they have to know her *heart*. But too many people know the history of this country — that 200 years ago we were slaves to the whites in power, and they couldn't see past the color of her skin. And it was hard for her, to face the looks of those who distrusted her, who despised her, not for anything she'd ever done, but for no reason at all. And yet, in the face of dislike, distrust and disinclination, she moved forward in what she was chosen by God to do, and she showed love and she showed faith, and she showed devotion, not only to the orphans, but to the *village* and its people. And it was somewhere in that first difficult year, when she was out there living at the orphanage, that she told me, "Miss Lynn, if I was to die, just bury me up on the mountain" and how do you question the dedication of someone from another place who will say *that*?

Now, these many years later, she's cruising. I paved the way, but she's *earned* the position she's in and the respect she's given.

FIFTEEN
A Matter of Grace

On one of my early travels up the mountain I went well past the lowlands where most people live, and headed up much higher, to visit the poorest of the poor, and in my trek I met an old man of 65 or 70 years-old named Kapi who was living under a rock. I know that sounds like a cliché, but it's the truth. His home was a cutout in a rock and it couldn't even be called a cave because it wasn't big enough *to* be called a cave. He was so dirty that he was more dirt than skin, he slept on a well-worn piece of cardboard and he had no shoes. Later, I brought him a pair and I don't think he ever wore them because he might not have *ever* worn shoes in his entire life. He was so skinny he looked like a frail twig, and he was extremely dark, he had a contagious laugh and always had a smile on his face. I'd bring him food and tried to talk him into coming down from the mountain so I could take care of him, but he wasn't going to leave what he'd known for perhaps his entire life. For all I knew, he'd *always* lived that way and to take him from that might have taken him from whom he *was*.

When you see a person living in a notch carved out of a rock, you understand that the grace of God is wherever people are living. It isn't just for people who go to church, or dress nicely or *think* they have a relationship with God, grace can be found in every corner and with all people. Grace was with Jonah in the belly of a great fish, it was with Peter when he denied Jesus not once, but *three* times, and it is with the people of Carries no matter what type of home they might be living in. When I saw some of the squalid places where people like Kapi were living, I knew there was no place where grace does not go. And it was with the realization that grace has no boundaries and is freely given because of God's unbounding love for us, that what I was only just starting to create with the blessing of God's love, was to be called 'Mission of Grace.' It was Kapi and those others I saw up on the mountain that made me realize, perhaps for the first time in my life, that God's love is perfection and the result of the sacrifice He made for us on the cross and in honor of that love, Mission of Grace came to be.

And even though I was only just starting the mission, and a bunch of children were in my care, I knew after meeting Kapi that it couldn't only be an orphanage, or simply for children, that whatever it was we were creating had to be something more and *in* that more there needed to be room to take care of the elderly because it was written in Isaiah 46:6 —

Even to your old age and gray hairs
I am he. I am he who will sustain you.

We'd hardly even gotten started and already the mission was quickly expanding, but without providence as a guide then what is the purpose of going forward?

When the children moved out of the little house and into the new orphanage, we immediately decided to keep the home we'd been renting and it would become an elderly home, and proceeded to turn it into such a place. How long does it take to transform a dwelling for the young to a dwelling for the old? – not long, we found out.

The little house was in the process of getting cleaned up when I was told of a woman who was living in a hovel and needed help desperately. I agreed to go and see for myself and someone took me to as poor a place as has ever been seen in Carries. Even I was shocked at the condition people were being forced to live and I hadn't fully understood the level of poverty that some had to face on a daily basis. The property I was taken to had a house at the front, although I'm not sure it could even be called a house. It was really just a straw hut and one had to duck to go inside the front door, except there was no door, just an opening to the inside of the shelter that was made of straw and looked like it would get blown down if I sneezed too hard. Living inside were four elderly men, two of whom were blind, and the third was nearly so. The fourth was somehow taking care of the other three, though at the most minimal level because no one had any money and they subsisted by begging or getting on by any means. All four were covered in dirt and were skinny from hunger. They bumped about in their tiny shack and were more than a little surprised that a visitor had been brought to see them. But despite the decrepit state of that shack, it was not the one that I had been asked to visit. Behind that was another and *it* is what I'd been brought to see.

I am easily humbled and I think that is a good thing, to be reminded of my blessings and that everything I have is only because God has allowed me to have it. *Stuff* is fleeting and could be gone with a great wind, but God's love for me is endless and does not change with the seasons. It is not a whim that rides on the winds. I was humbled when I was taken behind the blind men's shack and saw a place that was in even worse shape, not only in the condition of the dwelling, but for the way those who called it 'home' were forced to live.

The person I had been brought to see was a woman name Sinvlay, and she was the poorest woman I have *ever* seen in Carries.

Sinvlay's "house," and I use that term *very* loosely, was held up by just four large sticks and the covering atop was just a large dirty and oft-patched sheet, some bits of cardboard and maybe a piece of tin that were all held in place by a piece or two of rope and a prayer. Amazingly, Sinvlay lived it this house, although "tent" would be a more appropriate term, with five children and was pregnant with another. I have been in hundreds of houses in the community, but none were as bad as Sinvlay's.

I found out she was 35 years-old, but she could have easily passed for 60, and I knew immediately that something needed to be done. After that day I started bringing her food and put together a plan to get her out of such horrible conditions.

One day I went to see her and as we sat talking a chicken walked into the house and strutted around for a bit and then went over to the dirty mattress on the floor where the family slept and that crazy chicken proceeded to plop out an egg right on top of the mattress. Now I've seen a million chickens, and I've seen eggs, but never in all my years have I ever seen a chicken come in and blump-dee-blump an egg out on a mattress in someone's house, even if it's the worst house in town. And with *that*, I knew we needed to build Sinvlay a house.

Shortly after the chicken incident, Sinvlay went into labor and it was very difficult for her. Someone came and got me and Sinvlay gutted it out and willed the baby into the world right there in her little shack, and I witnessed that blessed event and even got to name the baby — Rachel.

Sinvlay led all of her children to Christ, even the oldest who was 15 when she was dedicated and all are active in our community today with Milani running our soup kitchen just down the hill from our church.

Through a lot of help and planning, the organization

called Team Haiti, led by my friend Miriam "Doodle" Cirotti, agreed to build a house for Sinvlay and it was going to be a blessing, but she would never live to see the house. She came home one night and complained that her arm ached and no one understood that that was a sign of a heart attack and she died in the morning. And it was so sad because she was so nice and active but so very poor. But still, Doodle had the house built and Sinvlay's family moved into it and it has been a blessing for them.

When the Elderly Home was ready to be opened I said to Jolem, "Go get Soma," a very poor woman I'd met high on the mountain who had children and grandchildren but they'd never been able to take care of her very well. Amazingly, she was 91 years-old, or so I was told, and she was the first person that we actually moved into the Elderly Home. She was tall, lively and smiled a grin that could melt a young man's heart, but she was a live-wire who had a devilish streak but was truly a happy person despite having very little.

The first man I brought to the Elderly Home came from the shack with four men, and I went and got one of those who was blind, a tall, frail and humble man named Villius. His care was not of the highest quality and I felt compassion for him and he has been living in the home ever since.

One of my favorite elders was a woman named Sé Marie who was so sweet, frail, skinny and loved the

Lord. She was over a hundred years-old when she came to live with us.[1] She'd been living with her children in Port-au-Prince and would often wander away from the house and happened to be gone when the earthquake hit. Sadly, she was spared but all her family members were killed when the house collapsed. My cousin found her wandering about in the streets and eventually brought her to me. I fed her spaghetti and she didn't even chew, she just swallowed it down whole and then I took her to the little home. She'd often ask for her children but I honestly don't think she ever realized they had died.

Marie had problems with her legs and walked about with two sticks that she used as canes, but whenever some guests would show up at the home, she'd sing and dance a crazy little dance and she loved to put on a show. I don't know how, but she lived to be 103 years-old, at least that's how old I was told she was, and when she died, she was the first that we buried in the Carries cemetery that is just a short walk from the orphanage.

Soma was the first who was brought to the home and she shared the front room with a woman named Sedonne. Sedonne had come to us when a seventeen year-old girl, who lived up in the mountains and

---

[1] One needs to be cautious when speaking to Haitians about their age. If someone says they are 71, they could easily have been *born* in 1971. They'll often throw out numbers when they have no clue. Many have no record of their birth and are uneducated and just don't know.

attended our church told us of about a woman who had no food, was always crying, seemed crazy and had lost her mind. "Can you bring her down?" I asked, and told her to bring another adult who could verify the story because so many times people made things up just so they'd get something for free. When she came down I knew the story was true—Sedonne was dirty and hungry and looked like she had Alzheimer's—and I took her in. Some days she knew everything and other days she knew nothing.

I was born in the village of Plaisance, high up in the hills at the southern end of Haiti and my mother still lives there. She called me up one day and told me that she had a woman she wanted me to take and because one does what mother asks, I went and got Sé Juliette. On first glance it appeared that she came to us with no pressing medical issues but within days she was going to the bathroom non-stop and became weaker by the hour. As it was, she had cholera and there was little we could do for her and she died in front of Miss Kim after having been with us for only a few weeks. She was the first of the mission's elders to die.

Because it is highly contagious, those who die of cholera are typically tossed into a common grave as quickly as possible and burned, but I would not allow this to be done to Sé Juliette. "Miss Kim, she is one of ours and I cannot allow her to be treated without dignity," I said, and so Miss Kim and I donned gloves and bathed Juliette and hers was the first dead body Miss Kim had ever touched. And we dressed her, and wrapped her in a blanket and all the time we prayed over her. And she was so frail that it was easy to pick up her body and place it in the coffin we'd provided, and then we took her to the cemetery and there was no doubt that despite being with us for only a short time, that she was one of ours, and as such, she was given the respect that we all deserve but do not always get.

A couple of weeks later, Soma, who was our very first resident in the Elderly Home, died and we held a nice funeral for her at the church. During the service, Sedonne was having problems with her legs and couldn't walk so I told the caregivers to take her back to the little house. She died the next day.

In two weeks we lost three of the elders.

Of course I was saddened by the deaths, especially for three in quick succession, but I took heart that those three died in a loving place and that in their final days they'd been cared for and loved, and each knew that Jesus had called them home to sit with him.

We rent the Elderly Home from a man who steadfastly refuses to sell us the property, and I don't blame him. We've made many improvements including a team from New York, led by Reverend Elan, building a separate kitchen. The little piece of property sits down a dirt path and apart from the rest of the mission. Soon enough, when the new Elderly Home is finished, those living in the house will have new and vastly improved environs to live out their days and we'll be able to expand to serve more than 30 instead of the handful we have today.

Besides Villius, Madam Tiffam was brought to church one day by a woman who told me that the Madam had a husband but he was handicapped and she was crazy, and after verifying the story, I took her in. She was so skinny you could wrap your fingers around her leg but she's almost fat now. We brought down her 25 year-old son, Odnal, who had a stroke and he lives in the house now, also.

John Claude is a young man who suffers from the effects of polio, a disease rarely seen anymore except in the poorest countries, and he is a godly who attends every service at the church and is quite the competitor at dominoes.

Madam Nikola is one of the more interesting people we've had live with us because she's a drama queen who's always fighting and cursing and hardly lives up to Christian ideals, and when I ask her if the reports of her crankiness are true she denies it to my face, although I've had numerous persons tell me of her indiscretions. She will deny her culpability until the cows come home, and as there are few cows in Carries she will be denying for a long time.

I told one of our missionaries about a 75 year-old woman, Lena, whose son had come to me to ask if we'd take his mother. "Why would I?" I asked and the man told me that he had a wife and five children, and his wife hated his mother and mistreated her — that she had her begging on the streets for food and that she was ill. I took Lena that day. I fed her and sent her to the hospital where she remained for seven days because her blood pressure was so high her head was going to explode.

Lena lived with us for over two years before she finally passed from cancer, and she died with dignity and with no pain. We had a nice funeral for Lena, too. We had a coffin made and we celebrated her life at church and then took her to the cemetery just down the hill from the Elderly Home.

The missionary I told this story to was moved and wanted to see Lena's grave and so I arranged for him to be taken and upon getting to the overgrown cemetery he found Lena's grave but it wasn't marked, and he went about marking it for her because, as he explained, the world should remember that Lena lived. It was a simple yet poignant little statement to a life that was worth living because Lena was a child of God.

If people ask why we do what we do, or why the Mission of Grace exists, all I'd have to do is tell them that all people are children of God and He expects us to take care of those who can't take care of themselves.

SIXTEEN
Bring the Water

For many in what we might consider the "civilized" world, it is hard to believe the extent that many must go to for even the most basic necessities of life. In Carries, water wasn't found at the end of a faucet that was plumbed into one's home because no homes had plumbing, or even doors or windows or anything other than a dirt floor. Toilets are most often holes dug into the ground, or not even that. For its entire existence up until that time, the getting of water in the village was had by going up and getting it. "Getting it" comprised of taking a bucket and climbing high up into the mountain and finding a trickling of water that might be smelly and nasty, but one isn't very discerning when you have to travel a half-mile up a mountain and down again with a five-gallon bucket on your head.

During the process of building the kid's home, a man named Joe Desrocher said to me, "This ministry must be real because I hear the children in the village shout your name" and I hadn't thought about it, but by seeing me amongst them, and on the dirt roads of the village, the hope and promise of God's love was leading me into the resident's hearts and minds and we were making a positive impact on the hill. Later, when

Joe himself saw what was happening and what blessings were being bestowed, he asked me what was our biggest need and I told him, "A baby house and water." We'd quickly outgrown our first building and needed another to separate our youngest orphans from those that were older and it was Joe who built that second building.

During construction Joe took notice of a young woman coming down the mountain while carrying a bucket of water on her head and he understood the need for water and even before the baby house was completed he was working on getting water down from up high on the mountain to where the people lived. It was no easy task, to engineer a system at the water's source, to create a huge cistern and a water pump, and to lay pipe to the dozen water spigots that were made and interspersed throughout the village. And the problems were often complex and annoying, made more so because it's *Haiti* where nothing is ever done easily and the hardships often make projects seem impossible. But nothing is impossible if God's presence is kept in mind and instead of taking directions from mere humans, we take our direction from Him.

The bringing of water down from the mountain was an important moment in the history of the village because it brought modernity to a place that hadn't ever had a modern notion, or so it seemed.

For thousands of years water has been used to symbolically represent new life, and certainly in

Christianity this is true, and the village was given new life, a baptism of sorts, when drops from crags formed and reformed to create a gauntlet, not of the water itself, but in what it *meant* for the future of a little village where modern life had finally taken hold in the form of some plastic pipes, concrete, valves, taps, sweat and the knowledge that in God, and in His infinite wisdom, those who put all the pieces together were working in His favor.

SEVENTEEN
A Place to Worship

I can never forget that I am the hands and feet of Jesus Christ and as His servant I am forever asking, "What is my purpose?" I never forget that what I'm living isn't my story — it's God's story and I am simply a vessel, or a conduit for what His power is. One day I will stop. One day God will tell me to stop or my body will give out and with Jesus' promise I will join Him in heaven, but God keeps going. When the hour is darkest, God is going strong. When the downtrodden and victimized cannot see even the hint of a glimpse of Jesus, God is going even stronger. Whatever infliction and shackle are keeping people from fulfilling the destiny that's been set before them can be broken by God's love. There is a resource at all of our fingertips that is far greater than any device that can be held in the palm of our hands and many times forgotten is the name of Jesus.

In my moments when I am tired or sick, when I'm dejected or bad-tempered, I sometimes think of Isaiah 6:8 —

> Then I heard the voice of the Lord saying, "Whom shall I send? And who will go for us?" And I said, 'Here I am. Send me.'

He said, "Go and tell the people."

The Lord brought me into this world and He will take me home one day. While I am on this earth awaiting that day, I hope that I will be of service and won't have a long interview at the Pearly Gates for what I *should* have done but *didn't* do.

One of the things the Lord might question me about is the mission's church, or lack of one. I didn't want a church and it was really for selfish reasons that one was built, although its addition to the mission was a Godsend and has been a foundational building block for the community.

In truth, none of the churches here in Carries were of my style and though I'd sometimes attend, it was not because I was drawn to them but it was out of some misguided obligation that I had to go *somewhere* on Sunday mornings. The idea of a church came from that seed. With the orphanage and the elderly home both up and running, and as we were becoming an establishment in the community, we needed to take a step in expanding not only the mission, but God's word, and the way to do that was with a church, and doing so would firmly plant my feet in the community and allow us to spread beyond the four walls of the orphanage and the little house that served our elderly friends.

Jolem is very much like me, although he is more of a diplomat than I could ever be. He is a voice in the community and knows the place and people much better than I ever will, and I went to him and said, "I need some land," and he took me around Carries and he showed me several pieces of property and then he took me to one on the side of a hill that was nothing but bush, brush and rock. But as we stood there on that rocky slope with the whole village spread out in a wide vista before us, and the blue ocean spread out even wider in an expansive display, in my mind I could imagine what would be built on that site. The fact it was just up the dirt road from the back gate of the orphanage made it a perfect place to set our roots even more firmly.

A couple of days later I went to the mayor of the area and told him what I was proposing to do and because I can be charming, persuasive and unpleasant all in the same breath, he sold me the land for less than it was really worth and on it we would build a church.

It wasn't a month or two later that Doodle came back to Carries and one of the first things I did was to take her up the hill to the new piece of property and she too looked over our terrain and said, "You don't need a church."

"No?" because that's exactly what I thought we needed.

And I don't know how Doodle's mind works, but she might be more of a visionary than I, but she saw what was *needed* when I saw what I *wanted*. "I'm going to build you a multi-purpose building," she said, and then we marched down the hill to the orphanage and she told me, "I'm coming back."

And when she came back our "church" had been funded, missionaries had been recruited as builders and it just seemed like that sort of thing happened every day, which it certainly did not in Carries.

To call our building a "church" is a misnomer even though that's exactly what people call the building. They call it a church even when grade school classes are being taught in it. They call it a church when community meetings are taking place in it. They call it a church when it's being used for everything that is not a church. But, on Sundays it's a church. And for weddings and funerals it's a church. And on Mondays and Tuesday nights when we have our men's and women's Bible studies, it's also a church. And it doesn't even have a cross on the outside, or on any of the walls inside, but when the band is kicking up, and the congregation is raising its voice in worship, or when the preacher is preaching, it most certainly is a church.

EIGHTEEN
Above the Clouds

They start out well before dawn from places that have no name and cannot be found on any map. They climb until they are above the clouds and at the crest they can look down over the valley below and the ocean beyond that stretches to the horizon. They might take a short rest there at the top, but more likely they keep trudging along.

The trails are well-worn as they've been travelled upon for centuries by the hill people and over the generations little has changed in their lives. Pick a date from the past and the populace of that time might still feel comfortable up in the hills because changes are so gradual they're hardly even noticed.

Those who travel for long hours are men and women of all ages, but mostly it's children who are carried or cajoled along hour after hour. They travel for the chance to see the doctor or a nurse in the clinic and will be given medicine if it's available, or they'll have to go up the highway to buy it if they have the time and money. Often they don't have one or the other or both.

It is those hill people who are most interesting because of how far they'll come and for their backstories; of how they wheedle out a living in an inhospitable place. But the clinic to which they're going is open to all and free to anyone who comes through the doors. Although it's plopped down in the corner of the village, it is open to people from Carries and beyond. If medicines are available, they're free, too.

People of the developed West, Americans in particular, would be surprised that all who come to the clinic put on their best clothes to do so. It is a point of pride among Haitians that to go see a professional, or to church, that one does so looking their best. Besides, since their outings are few, they might as well look good when stepping out. For a visit to the clinic, girls will be dressed in frilly dresses even if they have a large cyst on their neck that needs to be drained (as I once witnessed) and mothers might look as if they're going on a date. Grandmas will break out their shapeliest outfits and invariably men wear collared shirts and dress shoes.

A few months after the earthquake, a woman named Denise came to the gate of Ocean View with her little five year-old son. This young boy, so full of life and with a seemingly long future ahead, was having an asthma attack and gasped deeply because he could not breathe. Sadly, like Masaline, the boy died when he needn't have. The medicines needed to keep him alive are relatively cheap and available in nearly every clinic on earth, but as we had no clinic in Carries, he could not be saved and we were reminded again, in sad and heavy terms, that we were sorely lacking in even the most basic niceties of the 21st Century.

My conversations with Doctor St. Louis and his friends hadn't been in vain. Three years after its founding members had a *"prise de conscience"* (an awakening) when they made an unwavering commitment to making a difference in Haiti, their *Foundation for Hope and Health in Haiti* (FHHH) pledged not to forget the misery that the earthquake brought to the surface. And those involved realized that most of the post-earthquake relief was concentrated in Port-au-Prince while a multitude of people in need resided outside of the city. As such, a second trip to Carries at my invitation was made and subsequent visits were conducted to put on makeshift clinics. The teams were amazed by the long lines, the number of people who had never seen a doctor, the serious pathology, and the inability of the people to afford basic medical care.

Unlike many, they'd not only *wanted* to do something for the people of Carries, but they went out and *did* something. They held fundraisers and invited friends and others and they raised enough money to build the clinic, a white and green castle upon a hill, and then those same people stocked it and keep it stocked as best they can from Brooklyn. The clinic (*Centre de Santé de Carries*) has three examining rooms, a pharmacy, a procedure room with recovery area, and a waiting room. Over time, various medical teams have visited and have put on clinics or have simply worked in the clinic and have complemented our staff members and allowed for specialized care.

The clinic is not a big place, but more than 70 people are seen each day and no one will be able to recount how many lives have been saved because it's there, nor how much pain and heartbreak have been alleviated because of its presence in the community.

It is a diverse mix of the poor who trudge up or across the hill where the clinic sits. They arrive from the village, or lumber down from the mountains, or up the highway from Williamson, or down the highway from Montrouis, but they all come because there is something wrong and they hope that whatever ill they have can be fixed. And again, the mission gives hope that people will get better, and we pray that they do because that is our mission.

The people sit in the waiting room until their number is called and often the malady for which they come is an inconvenience and not life threatening. By far the most common problem is female infections, caused by poor water, poor bathing habits and poorer education. It is not something the women will die from but it can make their lives miserable and the clinic isn't just about saving lives, but of raising a standard of living.

Many, perhaps *most*, of those who arrive do so

because of maladies related to poor water, an all-too-common issue in Third World countries where clean water is a constant problem and is a fact that stops people from moving forward. If something as basic as clean water cannot be had, then what of food or education?

There are widespread beliefs that have been passed on from generation to generation that thwart people from moving forward. Common Haitian practices, particularly among women, are sometimes damning — why would women feel the need to wash themselves with *boiling* water after giving birth? Why do women believe that STD's can be caught from *other* men but not their *own*? What is considered "normal" in Haiti should often times not be. With education, lives will be made better. The clinic isn't just about saving lives; it's also about *improving* lives.

However, admittedly, most rewarding are those lives saved for the clinic having been raised. Preeclampsia is commonly diagnosed and without being so the women's and unborn child's lives are at stake. The prenatal care and medicines we provide make both mother and child healthier. The clinic has made a difference in innumerable lives, and though we've come far, we can go farther still.

NINETEEN
A Needed Break

Like the headlights of a car far off in the distance, I saw a fall coming long before it actually arrived. Of course, as a strong woman I didn't think it could happen to me so when it did, I was hit doubly hard. I was a superwoman who could not be stopped in whatever I wanted or needed to do, and I possessed the strength to carry on even when my mind was flagging. And even while I was wilting under the strain of the mission, the resort and all the ways I was being tugged, I still went on because that's what needed to be done. The hiring and firing, the ordering of food, budgets and finances, the children's health concerns, team visits, overseeing construction projects, resort guests, infrastructure needs, new orphans, interviews and on and on. One foot in front of the other, day after day, week after week, month after month.

For weeks I'd been asking myself why I was so tired. I no longer had to do things for myself, and yet, I was exhausted. I had cooks and drivers and house keepers and all these people who were taking burdens off my shoulders but my burdens only seemed to multiply. And as I wrestled with what was happening inside of me, and thought, "I can't do it anymore" I knew that I had to persevere because the mission was too important to leave and I'd run to my room and try to recharge my batteries.

But I never really ever got away. I might leave for a day or even a week, but I was in constant contact and every decision had to go through me and every bill had to be seen by me and everyone had to see me and there wasn't enough of *me* to go around.

I went to Port-au-Prince for a couple of days but when I got back to Ocean View I was overwhelmed with what needed to be done so I left again and went back to the capital where I tried to rest but it just wasn't working so I called Miss Kim and said we needed to go on vacation.

I had never been to Curacao and was looking forward to the visit, but on the plane I was like a zombie. I sat there with dark empty eyes and I could hardly hold my head up. I hardly had enough energy to walk off the plane. I knew I was really sick but I thought a week away would solve all my problems.

At the hotel, Kim was paying the cabbie as I went to the front desk to check us in, but when the man asked me my name I just looked at him and could not answer. "Are you okay?" he asked and I just shook my head. My mind had given out. I knew what my name was, and I knew why I was there, but I couldn't get the information from my brain to my lips.

We spent a week in Curacao but I never went out. I sent Kim out for some fun, but I just sat in my room and wrestled with my tortured brain. There was so much for me to do but I could not function so what was going to happen to what we'd built?

And after a week's vacation I felt even worse, because I realized something was severely wrong. Worst of all, I wondered if I could return to the mission, not just then, but ever again.

I went home, not to Ocean View, but to the States.

In Florida I saw my doctor who told me in no uncertain terms that I was to stay in America for no less than a month and then he'd see me again to reevaluate.

"I can't stay here for a month!" I argued. "There's too much to do."

"You won't be able to do *anything* if you're *dead*," he said caustically.

My brother, Jocelyn, brought me home from the doctor's office and told me, "What is the purpose if you just go back to die?"

I called my mother, whom I always turn to when my world seems to be falling apart, and her message was simple and something I should have realized already; "Miss Kim can handle it," mom said, and she was right.

For a whole month I stayed in bed and I had to drag myself out to use the bathroom. My brain just wouldn't function correctly and when I went and saw the doctor again he told me I was worse.

"How can that be?" I asked, and he told me that I hadn't even begun to rest.

I was cooking some eggs one morning and as I

looked at them boiling in a pot I knew they were ready but I couldn't get my mind and hands to work together to get them out. I kept staring at them and I told myself they had finished cooking, and I knew that the right thing to do was to take them off the burner, but I could not. I started crying and I wondered if my mind would ever work correctly again. I was found by my assistant and I could not fully explain what had happened and so I didn't even try.

For two months I couldn't step out of the house, and when I finally went to a mall with a friend to look at clothes it just seemed so pointless that I went home to sleep.

I was away from Haiti for five months.

Miss Kim and I were in constant contact throughout my recuperation. She wanted to keep me apprised of what was happening at the mission but without me having to tell her what to do. She was capable and didn't need to keep me informed, but it was out of respect that she did so.

When I came back, Miss Kim sat me down and said, "I watched my mom die, and I'll never go through that again." We had long talks about what I could and could not do, of what I should and should not do. She protects me, now. She stopped everything and took over. If there's a problem, I'm called in only if I'm needed, and often times, I am not. People who come looking for me have to go through her first, and many don't get through. People hate her because she protects me, but if I'd just returned to my old routine the same thing would have happened over again and it might have been even worse.

I lived a cautionary tale: Living on empty, you're going to crash.

TWENTY
The Baby House

At the orphanage there is a beautiful child, Eliza, who has large expressive bright eyes, a cherubic grin and for those lucky enough to get to know her a bit, a playful and loving heart. Her beginnings are inauspicious and sad for the commonness of her story. That she is at the orphanage, or even alive, is a gift from God.

Some of the details of where she came from, and how she came to us, might be different, but the *sort* of story is all too common in a country where life has often been a cheap commodity.

There is in Port-au-Prince the pleasant sounding *Cité Soleil*, a place that despite a beautiful name is extremely impoverished and densely populated and is regarded as one of the poorest and most dangerous slum areas in the entire world. In *Cité Soleil* there is garbage strewn upon garbage and virtually no sewers, but instead open canals serve as a sewage system for the population of 200,000 to 400,000 inhabitants. There are no government controls, the police will not enter and gangs have ruled the area for decades. Into that world, Eliza was born, although her life wasn't welcome and it was destined to be short lived.

A woman was walking in that harsh environment one day and stopped and looked at a teeming pile of garbage and was shocked to see a newborn baby setting atop the pile like a candle on a birthday cake. It was a newborn baby, a fact she knew because the girl was still wet, including her umbilical cord. And of course this woman just couldn't leave the child in a pile of garbage to die, or to be killed by wild dogs or feral pigs that also dwell in that filthy place, so she took the baby and brought it to my cousin who does social work in *Cité Soleil*, and later that day the baby, Eliza, was brought to me and she became my charge. By coincidence and divine conjunction, two days after her arrival a woman from Atlanta came to visit the mission as she sometimes does, and fell in love with the three day old Eliza and has been working to adopt her ever since.

Eliza's is a good story right out of the movies, except it's real and hers is a story of life from near certain death. A middle-aged man, who came and spent several months with us, once spoke of the mission as being about life and death, and I'd never looked at it in those harsh terms, but in many respects, he was right. He once asked me how many of the orphans and elderly would not be alive if our mission did not exist, and I thought two-thirds, or roughly 40 individuals, was a truthful answer. This middle-aged man used that figure in another conversation when arguing (though not argumentatively) a point. "If you don't think it's about life and death," he told the man he was conversing with, "*you* choose the 40 children who would not be here today if the mission didn't exist."

I tend to think of the mission in terms of *life*, that is, the lives we have, the ones we are growing, nurturing and furthering for the benefit of God, mankind and Haiti. That is not to say that death isn't a part of the story, because it is, and for all those who die in our community we want them to go with the knowledge and love of Jesus Christ whose promise of heaven is the building block of why we believe.

There were too many stories like Eliza's. In Haiti there are roughly 300,000 orphans, or 3 out of every 100 people, and though there are many orphanages, there are not enough and certainly not enough with our mission statement—to educate and raise future leaders that will represent Jesus well.

Because there are too many stories like Eliza's, and we had no room to accept more children, we did what came only naturally, or seemed proper—we built another orphanage and moved in our littlest children. The new building allowed us to more than double our occupancy and we now have more than 60 children in our care with ages that range from six months to 12 years.

By no stretch were our orphanage ministries completed by the addition of a new building, instead we look ever upward for opportunities that

God is calling us to be a part of even if they don't fall under the umbrella of the Mission of Grace.

Not a quarter-mile up the hill from ours is another small orphanage that we've adopted and have started to assist with food and water, to say nothing of the missionaries we often send over to just love on the kids and to provide manpower for projects that are needed. With 16 children in a two room building that was without doors, beds or storage, and funded by a benefactor to the tune of just $30 a month, the pastor works tirelessly for those orphans in his charge and we've come to their aid with the necessities of life, but also in raising the standard of the building itself. All of the children now sleep on beds, they are better clothed and better fed, they go to the clinic more often and their overall health has improved immeasurably. It has been a blessing to be involved in something so near to our own ministries and we are happy to be reaching further out into the community.

We have taken even bigger steps than to just minister to those close to our own doorsteps.

A whole book could be and should be written about my parents and the ministry they started and nurtured in Plaisance Sud, where I was born. Another book could be written about how my brother, Jocelyn, has taken that ministry and grown it far beyond what even my parents could have imagined. And because of a need in Plaisance, we at the Mission of Grace decided to contribute to what was happening there by partnering in the opening of an orphanage. In a scant two years the home has grown to house fifteen children. The orphanage and the village's clinic (a part of the Guillaume Foundation started by my parents) are overseen by Ryan and Jill Dolan, who in a calling by Christ moved from Washington state to Haiti with their seven children and have ingratiated themselves into the village and with the people. Aside from their "official" duties, as residents who live in the heart of the community, they assist many families with food, they're a support system for dozens of residents and are examples of Christian ideals of love, marriage and family.

We are proud to have been asked to be a part of the movement in Plaisance since it is where I was born, where my father's influence is still felt, and where my brother has been a well-respected presence in the community for nearly twenty years. And like in Carries, there is a plan in Plaisance, too, to expand out of the old small building that the orphans live in today, to a much larger and more modern facility that will be a further springboard to the future.

TWENTY-ONE
The Teen Home

Beautiful names are one of Haiti's biggest assets. It is unfortunate that names cannot be sold on the open market because Haiti would be a world leader in such a practice. As it is, the country is instead a leader in poverty and the manufacture of t-shirts.

The girls in our Girl's Home are not lacking in beautiful names: Nata, Odline, Eliane, Elitane, Bethanie and Rachelle to name a few. They are the type of names that get passed down from one generation to the next. Though modern conventions might be prideful in taking names from popular culture, it is those names that have been a part of the historic *Haitian* culture that ring and resound most loudly. I am Linotte, a name that has fallen out of favor but was cast and steeped in what Haiti was, but is as much a part of that as what Haiti *can* be.

We'd long had the idea to take girls and boys off the streets and to offer an alternative to life's minimal possibilities that can be found in the community. Sadly, for young women, poverty, early pregnancy and prostitution are prevalent up on the hill and are not only distinct possibilities, but probabilities. When one has little food it is hard to say what one should or should not do to fill the belly. Carries is simply a microcosm of the rest of Haiti and just because we have a thriving mission in the village, one should not assume that all problems are fixed or will be fixed any time soon. It is our desire to rid the world of all ills and pains and to harness people's strengths and to minimize their weaknesses, but we are a work in progress.

Our girl's home started out as no girl's home at all, just a need and a willingness on my part to try to do for some girls what wasn't being done for them at home. I wanted them to be educated and taught Christian values and a work ethic that is all too rare with the vast majority of young people in Haiti.

Leana was the first, and it wouldn't be fair to call her a guinea pig but sometimes that's what the first are. She was a moppet, really, just a skinny little waif who I'd seen throwing rocks on the beach at Ocean View. She'd come around several times and in her I recognized a far-away look of someone seeking something greater, or at least better than what she was living in.

One day I watched her out on the beach and I'd seen enough, not that I was angry but more curious than anything else. I walked down to the beach and asked, "What are you doing here? Why aren't you in school?"

She sort of shrugged and didn't give me a straight

answer and because I'd seen her just hanging around I said, "Go get your mother."

"Why?" she asked.

"Because I want you to live with me" I said and she left. Later that day, as the sun started to set, her mother showed up at Ocean View's gate with Leana trailing behind. We sat down on the patio and her mother explained that she had six children at home and was having a tough time of it, and then she nodded at Leana and said, "Please take her, she's always in the streets getting into trouble."

Several people told me not to take Leana, that she would be more trouble than she was worth, and that in the village she had a reputation, and though she was only fourteen, she was already with men, but I didn't listen to any of that idle blather and I took her, and not as some girl in my charge, but as my daughter. I don't just say that as a passing comment, I say it for the truth behind the words. She is as much a daughter as the daughter I gave birth to. When I get angry at her, it is with the anger of a mother who is trying to teach her daughter the ways of righteousness, and when I impress my love upon her it is with the pounding heart that only a mother can know.

Leana was the first but when word got out I quickly found four more and the five were living at the resort and eating healthily for the first time in their lives, and they were going to school, most for the first time in their lives, and in a short period of time their lives and prospects *for* their lives had turned around.

When my friend Doodle was here for one of her visits she saw what I was doing, and who I had and she said, "Miss Lynn, you can't have girls just living there."

"Why not?" I asked.

"Because it's not right."

I wasn't concerned with what people *thought* was right, I wanted to *do* what was right. "I need to take care of them," I said.

Doodle shook her head and thought I was crazy. "I want to build you a house," she said and I thought that was just about the best idea yet.

I am blessed to be part of a community of friends and family throughout the world that believes in doing something and not waiting around for something to happen. It didn't take long for the word to spread that we were proposing to build a house for the girls of the community and a Canadian woman, Esther Cram, sent five thousand dollars to get us started.

Miss Kim and I debated where the house should be located and we decided it would be easier to keep track of what was going on if the house was in the same walled compound as the orphanage and so that's where it was to be built. We cobbled together some plans and it wasn't to be anything fancy or elaborate, and would be very much like the other buildings in the orphanage.

Once that decision was made *to* build, Miss Kim suggested that we shouldn't start construction until we had all the money, but I didn't want to wait. When she left the country for a couple of weeks on a speaking tour, I told Jolem to dig a foundation and by the time Kim came back we had it finished. Miss Kim doesn't like to leave the mission because she often feels as if she's missing out on what is happening. She never knows what it's going to look like when she returns and knows that in her absences I take the opportunity to build, or tear down, or to do *something*. This is not to say that she doesn't approve, and thankfully she never has been one to say, "Miss Lynn, we should wait until we have a plan, or money" because what are plans or what is money when doing God's business? That is not a statement of flippancy because there is no opinion I trust more than Miss Kim's, and when I have important decisions to make concerning the mission, I always consult with her, but sometimes God moves in ways few can perceive.

Once we had a foundation, Doodle once again stepped in and with several thousand dollars she'd raised, we raised walls, and then Steve Erickson came from Canada with a team to put on a roof and then girls were moving into the house. It all happened very quickly and it has been a blessing to have the house in the community with the orphans, and it is a blessing to have them in the mission. It is a blessing to see them growing and expanding into womanhood and into positions of importance and leadership, not only with us, but with this country and this world. That might sound like an overstatement, but it is what I believe and what I *know*.

Being a woman, I take very seriously the challenging issues the young women of our community and in my country face each day. The expectations that are placed on them, and the burdens they must bear, are often more than what they can carry. As important as it is that we're providing a safe haven for the orphans, that we've taken this handful of young women and are offering them a future far above and beyond that which they would have otherwise is a blessing.

The young women of our house have different stories and backgrounds, but their futures shine brighter because they've been chosen to live with us, and that is a very important distinction. Unlike the orphans, who we've been given, the young women have been invited and as such there are expectations that one requires.

One of the girls was sneaking out at night to meet with boys, something girls have been doing since the beginning of time, but she'd forgotten her blessing. She was there because she'd been chosen, and that her future was going to be brighter because she'd been given the opportunity. But teenage girls don't realize what they have. Nor do they realize the value of avoiding sin. As punishment for her indiscretions, she had to live with Miss Kim for a month, as if that was the worst thing in the world. But she was away from her friends and she had to work, and take care of Miss Kim's sons and I hope she learned a lesson much larger than 'don't get caught while sneaking out in the middle of the night to meet with boys.'

I could go on forever about each of our young women, but a note on a few will suffice to get the point across of what we're building in them and for Haiti from a disparate and eclectic mix:

Suzie's mom was blind and couldn't control her daughter who was always on the streets getting into all sorts of trouble, and I wanted to save her. She is extremely smart and is number one in her class. She is also a rarity in that she is a quick learner and understands things the first time.

Marta is an ingenious young woman who is always thinking of ways to make money and is going to be an entrepreneur or a businesswoman of some sort and has the chance to go far. I imagine that all of us will be working for her someday.

Rose's mother came to me and said, "I have a daughter and she's very bad."
    "No, she cannot be too bad" I said.
    "She loves the boys and got pregnant. Take her," she said to me with a wave of her hand, and I took Rose so she could learn a better way while the baby is with her

mom.

Wildé was from far up the mountain and when she hadn't shown up at school for six weeks I went to find out why.

"What happened to Wildé?" I asked her mother.

"She's sick" I was told, so we sent her to a doctor in Port-au-Prince.

She came back and was doing much better, but when I hadn't seen her at church one Sunday I sent a woman up the mountain to bring Wildé's mom down. I was surprised when I was told that Wildé had received a voodoo spell. "Then give her to me" I said quite casually because I know all that voodoo blather is just a bunch of crazy talk and I'm in the business of saving people in the name of Jesus and am not intimidated by a bunch of grandma hoodoo voodoo garbage.

Her mom kind of sloughed me off and said, "If you can save her, take her."

I don't know what was wrong with Wildé but I sent her to live at the grandma's house and we prayed over her and after about four weeks of constant care she started to get better and whatever stupid voodoo spell they think had been gripping her in chains was broken by the power of Jesus and love.

As of this moment we have fifteen girls and only one cannot read and write and we've saved an untold number from getting pregnant or from selling themselves. We have one basic goal in the house, that they have other options than having to coax a hard life from the earth.

TWENTY-TWO
A New Home for Men

As a woman, I felt I had a vested interest in the young women of the community, and as we were concerned and moving along with *that* ministry, my son, Don, came to me one day and asked, "Mom, what will happen to the boys from the orphanage when they grow into men?" Truthfully, it was something we'd given thought to, but only in the vaguest of terms and we'd never done anything to definitively answer the question. It was Don who attempted to find a solution to the continued presence of the young men who will move on from the orphanage, but also for young men in our community who might be at-risk.

Even as Don was giving definition to the possibilities, he started working with an organization that offered to build not only a small home for men, that we now call The Men of Grace, but also a building that could be used for a multitude of purposes — training, manufacturing, education, assembly and more. And though both buildings were built, the crush of many other projects and ministries, along with the lack of a man in the mission to oversee the ministry, has stopped us from moving ahead fully, but when God's perfect timing is upon us, we'll be blessed to have a foundational facility that will offer hope and possibility where little existed before for men in the community.

It is painfully obvious that unemployment runs rampant in Haiti and to train young men will give them an upper hand in the future when seeking employment. Like every impoverished area of the world, jobs are scarce in Haiti and anything that will give someone an advantage in getting a job or retaining one will be a huge benefit. As such, The Men of Grace uses Proverbs 22:6 as its principle:

Train a child in the way he should go,

And when he is old he will not turn from it.

In adopting that credo we hope to continue discipleship in Christian values and to provide a trade center to grow not only technical skills (carpentry, plumbing, masonry and electrical) but additional skills such as computers.

TWENTY-THREE
Goodbye, Kapi

I have long known that human nature often coerces us to do dumb things. That should not be a revelation but simply a reiteration or a caution to avoid those things in life that will cause us harm, dismay and destruction. Our ability to get ourselves into trouble when it can easily be avoided seems to be inbred in us; it's been that way since the beginning of time and you'd think that we might have understood some of our fallibilities and tried to correct them, but we keep making the same mistakes over and over. It is said in America, that those who do not know history are doomed to repeat it, and that truism is good everywhere on the globe. The mudslide that essentially started the Mission of Grace in 2009 should have been a lesson but lessons are often hard learned in Haiti. Just as soon as the mud of that slide dried up, people went back to building houses right in the slide's path and all seemed well and good until a sunny day in 2015 that turned bad.

It was late in the afternoon and Miss Kim had just left for a month-long vacation in Canada. It had been a sunny day with intermittent clouds that would have caused no one even a moment of concern. Even when the clouds darkened and the rains came no one was overly concerned, not even when they started falling heavily. They were heavy, but not the worst, and a group of missionaries had no trouble getting to Ocean View for the start of their week stay. Dinner was served, rooms were assigned and we even had a little orientation meeting for those who'd never been before.

At 8:30 at night, my son, Edwin, came to my room and told me that people in the village were leaving their houses because of the rains and that he'd brought three ladies with new babies to the resort and was going to feed them and give them dry clothes. That's the type of person he is, someone who will go out of his way to help another. While getting the women, Edwin found five more whose houses were flooded and he brought them to Ocean View as well.

We fed all the women and gave them dry clothes and everyone went to their rooms except for Edwin who went about rescuing in the village.

At 10:30 there was a knock on my door and the resort's overseer, Camillo, told me that there'd been a mudslide and that it had knocked a hole in the wall and I needed to get out. "A hole in *what* wall?" I asked, and I was informed that part of Ocean View's wall had come down.

Camillo put me on his back and in the dark of the night he carried me through the mud and water that was filling the resort and placed me on a wall where I would be safe.

I was crying because I know what had happened five years prior across the road, and slowly the missionaries all came out and told me they were safe, and many of the employees found me to tell me they were also safe but they also informed me that the whole resort was mud-filled and several of the rooms were filling with mud and gunk. But even before the mud had stopped flowing, people were getting to work. They were sweeping the mud down toward the beach or into the ocean. They were using every tool imaginable to get it from here to there. And it was a blessing that even in the dark people were doing God's work.

Two ladies spent the night with me and when I awoke in the morning I was devastated at what I saw. It appeared as if the resort was in ruins with three feet of mud everywhere. But in a show of oneness with the mission, and with me, people started showing up to clean Ocean View and amazingly, road equipment was sent by the government to clear the highway out front. We were blessed to have the right team here, Team Haiti, and they jumped right in, and over the next few weeks we had missionary teams show up from California and from Tennessee to help with the cleaning. Although it took nearly five months before the mess was completely cleaned up and to get things back to normal, it was a lesson in what can happen with a community spirit and what can happen when people have a common goal. The cleaning up was very much like the mission itself — there was a problem and people got together to solve what the problem was. And it will take a lot more than mud that was sent by the damnable devil to foil our advances.

Sadly, three people died in the mudslide; two young boys and Kapi, he who lived in a rocky outcropping far up the mountain and refused to move down no matter how many times either Miss Kim or I tried to get him to come to the mission so we could take care of him. His body was found bent and broken as it had been washed far down the valley from his home.[1]

On the Sunday after the mudslide we went to church by making a path out of the resort, and we remembered those who'd died, and we prayed for those who'd lived, but most of all we prayed for guidance and mercy in the face of adversity. We might never understand God's plan, but we're confident that even in the worst of times He is near with a loving and open heart. And it is sometimes hard to remember that he doesn't protect us *from* the storm, He protects us *in* the storm.

---

[1] Kapi's death touched Miss Kim in particular. She'd often take Joshua and Josiah up the mountain to visit and she had a spiritual kinship with him. When she speaks of Kapi it is always with a smile on her face and a hint of remorse that she couldn't have done more to help him.

TWENTY-FOUR
A Continuing Story

I often get far more credit than I deserve, and though this is my book, I do not want to make it seem that I have done more than I have.

For a long time Miss Kim lived at the orphanage and was its director. As we grew so did her place and position in the mission. It is she who has gone out far more than I to speak and spread the word about our story and the mission. She has spoken at dozens of churches and told our story hundreds of times and always with the enthusiasm of someone who believes in what that story *is*.

And yet, despite all Miss Kim has put into the mission, and the sacrifices she's made to bring it to where it is today, I am fully cognizant that people hate her because she is trying to set and uphold a standard, because she sometimes has to say "no," and because she protects me. And though she was not born in this country, if you sit in a bakery you're going to smell like bread, and she is as much Haitian as me, even if she sometimes cannot understand what her two sons are saying because their Creole is better than hers. And for all she is, and for all she has done, still, to put her into a position of influence and power far beyond just the orphanage's walls seemed mistaken to some, perhaps many. Has she always been right or correct? I don't know any of us that have. Has she stumbled and sometimes fallen? Haven't we all. I don't expect anything from Miss Kim beyond what I know she is capable of, and she is capable of a great deal.

Having lived in the orphanage and so closely to those original children, it was difficult for Miss Kim to move out and to hand over the reins to someone new, but as she's taken on larger responsibilities, not only in the mission but at Ocean View, she's done so with dexterity and wisdom.

Two women showed up one day and told me in no uncertain terms that they wanted me to take their babies. I looked at both of the children and said, "These children are healthy. I wouldn't take them even if we had the room, which we do not." But both were insistent that they were incapable of taking care of their children when I knew otherwise; all they needed was some support and encouragement. I told them to return in four days at which time I'd not only have a place for their children to live, but a place for them to live, also.

We have several houses throughout the community and I knew that one of them was being vacated shortly and told some of our employees to make it available for the women as quickly as possible. When the two women arrived on the appointed day, we moved them into our new Single Mothers Home and another joined them just a day later. In three days we'd created a new ministry.

When there is a need, there is also a need to *do* something. I am loath to sit around and plan and to give a lot of thought when action is needed and if God gives His blessing then I am of the mind that He wants something done in a timely manner. Haiti is a beautiful place for many reasons, but one is because things can happen quicker than in other parts of the world. With no government interference then there doesn't need to be the endless haggling that weighs people down so inaction rules the day. This is not to say that we are foolish with our energy, time or finances, because we are not.

For all that the Mission of Grace is, and for all it does, perhaps the most important aspect is the school. With a proper education many other things fall into line and the possibilities are endless. When we opened our school we ran out of room about ten minutes later, and with tender mercies a new one is being built. At some time in the future, 350 students will be enrolled at our school and all of them will be attending free of charge. We are expanding our sponsorship program to alleviate our costs but nonetheless, the burden is squarely on our shoulders if the need arises, but our shoulders are stout and our belief is strong. And we believe God will find an answer for our needs.

During the early construction of the new school, Jolem came to me to say that additional money was needed. "What for?" I asked, because I thought we'd budgeted everything down to the last gourde. He then told me that a form made out of rebar had been stolen during the night.

"No one saw anything?" I asked suspiciously, not of Jolem whom I trust implicitly.

"No," said Jolem.

"It would have taken four men to carry that form away, so someone must know what's going on."

"If anyone does, they're not saying."

I gave the moment some thought and bided my tongue, something I am not happy to do and rarely will. Finally, I said, "Ah, so we can be stolen from and no one will care? Is that how it works?" but it was a question that I didn't expect Jolem to answer. "I'm not doing payroll until the rebar is found" I stated angrily and sincerely.

"What?" asked Jolem.

"No one will be paid until the form is found," I said with renewed vigor. "Someone knows what happened, and because it's going to hurt *their* pockets, they'll do what's right."

By 5:00 o'clock that afternoon the form had been returned and the guy who had stolen it was sent away. I don't even know what "sent away" means, and I don't think I want to know, but I made my point. We are here for the community, and we are a part of the community, but we are not a free ride for all. If we were, then there would be no self-reliance and we'd simply be a charity. We don't want all of ours to simply have a free ride from birth to grave. That is not the purpose nor is it healthy or Biblical.

I always thought that the writing of a book was merely throwing a lot of words into a blender and mixing them up until they made sense. That is a rather un-writerly view of a craft that I will never master. However, with God as my guide, and with the assistance of others, this book is being written. It's almost a miracle. In writing a book I had about the same sense as starting an orphanage, or a school, or an elder's home, but all of those have come to fruition. We are not a community of people in a little village, we are a community of *man* with arms spread wide and willing to take in all people.

TWENTY-FIVE
A New Home on the Hill

There was an elderly lady, Madam Rose, who was tiny as a mouse with a heart of gold. She'd lived with us for nearly two years when it was announced that we were going to build a new Elderly Home. Though very sick with breast cancer, and in great pain, it was Rose's desire to live long enough to move into the home. As the disease ravaged her body and sapped her strength, we finally had to move Rose to a hospice outside Port-au-Prince where she died without ever having seen the raised walls of the new home.

By contrast, Madam Tiffam is silent now from a stroke, but always with a wide smile on her face that belies a richness in her brain that cannot escape in words. Day after day, week after week, for three years she sat in the same place in her wheelchair on the porch of the Elderly Home. In early 2016 she was joined by her 25-year-old son, Odnal, whom we brought down from the mountain after he too suffered a stroke. From her appointed spot, Tiffam kept an eye on three of the scraggiest looking dogs one can imagine, who lolled about on the small property, or she eyed the few goats that roamed about and watching them get into trouble can be amusing entertainment. She watched the men playing dominoes outside the kitchen not fifteen feet away from where she sat, and she watched the world go up and down on the dirt road that bypasses the home, but there are few passers-by. Although it is not a lush spot on Carries' landscape, it has a dappled sort of lushness and there are olive green trees and shrubs that are typical of the village, though few look healthy or inviting. It's not the worst place in the world to let time pass by, but neither was it the best, although it's a far cry from that which Tiffam lived far up the mountain in the nether reaches of what might be considered the village, a place where the landscape becomes nearly wild and untamed, although that could describe most of Haiti, including all of its cities. Her previous home, where some of her family still lives, is a palm-frond and cardboard roofed lean-to with a floor scraped bare of rocks and walls that are hardly suitable to keep the elements or anything else out. The front door is an old women's dress that is suspended from some rusted wire woven through the shoulder straps.

The Elderly Home had seven living in it, all crammed into a space that allows enough room for their beds and little else. The bathroom is out back behind some rusting pieces of tin and some broken pieces of rotting wood that give only the barest sense of privacy as people go about their business.

Of the others who called that place home, Villius tended to find a seat by the front gate that was held closed by a rusting chain that appears to have been found, or stolen, from elsewhere in the mission. He sat cross-legged as a sentry, though his blindness would make him about the worst sentry one could imagine.

Madam Nikola also tended to find a seat near the gate, usually right outside so she can be the first to see visitors, but she rarely spoke to them and kept her eyes cast downward when spoken to. She tended to sit in the dirt or on a rock and not in a chair for reasons no one had asked and it might simply be her preference. She often fell asleep there out front, resting peacefully in the shade and sometimes you would see someone step closely to watch and to see if she was still breathing or if she has expired.

As I sometimes sat with the elders, I wondered what would be lost when they moved into the new home and if what they gained would outweigh the loss. There is something of a quaint charm to the small house that will be lost, but with size we'd be able to accommodate so many more and it will be a building block to the future of the community.

One of the missionaries pointed out to me that he thought it was interesting all that Madam Tiffam would be able to see as she sat up in the new Elderly Home, that we officially named the Home of Grace. And he took me up to the porch of the home as it was being built and we looked down off the hill and out over a wide and sweeping valley and we pointed out various places of interest. There was the school a hundred yards below, and three houses on our property to say nothing of those homes that rimmed the periphery, and there were the outer reaches far beyond where the village thinned out. Each day many children pass by while going to or coming home from school. Many people pass by on the way to the clinic just up the hill. We pointed out the Baptist church some half-mile away. And we looked out over the ocean with its sailboats and the ferry that ran from La Gonâve fourteen miles distant, and the waves and changing pattern of the clouds. And if you know where to look, and if you look closely enough, you can see the village's cemetery far off in the distance, and you can make out the tombs and that is where Madam Tiffam will be buried one day, and it is where Madam Rose is buried, she who did not live long enough to see the new home built.

And all that was soon to be in Madam Tiffam's hands as she sat in mute silence on the patio of her new home.

We cannot change the whole world, but we can change a little piece of it, and if a million people, or a billion people, or *seven* billion people could change little things then think about the possibilities. For today, I'll suffice with the fact that with the new Home of Grace we're going to change one person's world — Madam Tiffam's, and that's a pretty good day's work.

In April 2016, a dream four years in the making finally

came true. It was something we'd prayed about too many times to imagine and it was too long in coming, when we moved not only the seven from our Elderly Home, but an additional seven as well, into the grandest building in all of Carries, the Home of Grace. On the appointed day, those that could walk the half mile to the new home did so, and it was no small feat to get eighty year-old women over the dusty roads and up the hill to their new home, but it was done with a sense of great expectation and love. Women and men you never would have expected to make such a trek were joined with others in a joyous procession. And when the residents were sitting on new rocking chairs on the patio, and as my husband said a prayer to Jesus in thanks for all He'd provided, it was a tearfully joyful moment to once again see God's power at work — to see what He is capable of doing. We had wanted the home to be built much sooner, but in the end the timing was perfect because we'd waited for God to inform us as to when we should proceed and we followed His timeline.

There are thousands of orphanages in Haiti, some large and some very small, but there are virtually no homes for the elderly who are often shamefully cast aside like some of ours had been, and by making a statement in such a grand edifice for the elderly, the promises of God are shown to the entire village.

TWENTY-SIX
Stories of Grace

For we who labor each day at the Mission of Grace, it is not difficult to remember why we do so. However, if our purpose ever slips our mind, as a reminder all we have to do is walk over to the orphanage and look into the face of almost any one of the children and it is not difficult to conjure up a story that is often similar to another but also different in its own right, just as each child is different.

It is not a stretch to say that all of the children are saved, and if that means they are "saved" in the eyes of God then that would be fine enough, but I am not one who can make that assessment, all I can say is that they are alive when often they would not be and thus they've been saved from an early grave. The rest I put into God's hands.

Our beginning was about children, and though we believe every Haitian life has a positive purpose ordained by God, it is the children who are the future. Ours are being raised to be Haiti's leaders and we are teaching them to love others, to have morals and ethics and to remind them that they are representatives of Jesus.

Almost by definition, orphans have backstories that

make us pause and reflect or pause to weep. Not all of our children have lost their parents, on the contrary, more than half were given to us by parents who could not support their own. We offer prayers on a daily basis for all of our children, that they will be blessed by God and have been given hope in the name of Jesus. And it is our belief and dream that all of our children will one day make a difference.

I don't like to dwell on where our children have come from or why they are given to us, but the stories are as much about Haiti as they are the individuals and a purpose for why we exist as a mission: to change Haiti and to make it a better place.

Daniel's single young mom came to our gate three times to give him away. The first time we sent her home with milk and diapers and told her she was capable of taking care of him with some support. The next week she returned and he was wheezing so we gave her money to take him to the hospital. The doctor told her to stop breastfeeding because she was not eating properly and it was affecting her baby. When she returned a third time, when Daniel was two months old, we kept him.

Several months after giving birth, Lisette's 17 year-old mother realized she was incapable of taking care of a fragile little baby. When she was given to us, Lisette weighed only half as much as a baby her age should weigh and was tragically thin. Sadly, she was disengaged from people and her surroundings and still carries a forlorn sort of countenance even after all these years.

Gina is the youngest of eight children. When her father died suddenly her mother was having a tough time keeping all the children fed. Gina was two months old when she came to us and was severely malnourished. Her mother also brought two other sons hoping we'd also take them, but they were relatively healthy and we only take the worst of the worst.

Yolene's mentally-challenged mother got pregnant from having been raped. Upon being born, Yolene was left on her grandmother's doorstep, but with eight children to take care of already, the grandma gave Yolene to us when she was just ten days old. She was very small and remains underdeveloped to this day.

When Lucia's mother brought him to the orphanage, he was severely malnourished, emaciated and lethargic. Because of his malnourishment he wouldn't engage anyone. We knew immediately that if we did not take him he would soon be dead and his mother didn't care if he lived or not, so the decision to leave him with us was an easy one to make.

Jonas' father left his 23 year-old mother just as soon as

she informed him of her pregnancy and eight days after giving birth she died from complications. The father wanted nothing to do with the baby and with no one else to care for him, Jonas came to us.

A lady was walking on the island of La Gonâve, fourteen miles distant from Carries, and heard the sound of cats mewing in an abandoned home. Thinking it strange, she went to investigate and found a wooden box with a rag on top, and when she pulled off the rag she found not kittens, but Sonia and Rubens, twin sisters. The woman took the children, who turned out to be just 15 days old, and found their mother who was too overwhelmed with the twins and her two other children and felt that abandoning them was her only choice. She refused to take the girls back and the woman found the twins' father, who'd abandoned the family some months before, and he too wanted nothing to do with the twins. The woman knew about our mission and took the ferry over and when we got them both girls were very small and sick because they'd been eating nothing but boiled crackers for ten days.

All of our children have stories, and it doesn't matter where they come from, or how they got here, we are just thankful to God that we are blessed to have been entrusted with their care.

TWENTY-SEVEN
A Kite Story

There is a spirit of chaos in Haiti that is both exhilarating and exhausting, but in the turmoil, there are small moments that make one pause and smile.

In the village there are always kites flying. On any given day they're in the sky and we hardly even notice their presence. It is always boys flying the kites, but girls and men and women and old women and old men should every once in a while, too, because it will keep us forever young by reminding us of the joys of youth that are often forgotten as we wrinkle and turn gray.

What I love about the kites of the village is that they're not store-bought, they are made from found sticks that are tied together and overlaid with a found garbage bag or a little plastic sheet. Tails are often made from discarded pieces of cloth and the string is sometimes unwoven from an old piece of clothing and wound around a stick or an old can. Despite how they're made, the kites fly majestically.

There is something beautiful about a place where kids make their own kites and fly them as if they're free birds on the winds floating effortlessly up in the heavens.

TWENTY-EIGHT
Inhumanity

There is a pretty seven year-old girl, Andiana, who comes from just outside of Carries, and as punishment for drinking his bottle of juice, her father took Andiana's hand and held it over an open fire until it was charred. I don't like to think of the pain poor Andiana must have experienced for her indiscretion, and I don't like to think about what sort of man would do something so terrible to anyone, let alone his daughter.

Andiana came to our clinic but there was little we could do for her there, so we paid to have her sent to the hospital in Saint Marc. The doctors did all they could, but despite their best efforts, too much damage had been done and Andiana's fingers had to be amputated.

While the mother was at the hospital, the father called and told her in no uncertain terms that if she did not come and get their three other children, he would pour gasoline over their heads and light them on fire. Needless to say, we rescued the family and moved them into our single mother's home.

Man's inhumanity was not born in Carries nor is it only available in Haiti — it is a problem in every corner of the globe. But just because it is a fact of life does not mean that we have to stand idly by and watch it happen, instead we want to be active participants so it doesn't happen again. We do not accept inhumanity but we accept the challenge of Jesus to take care of those who cannot take care of themselves and to rid the world of injustice.

Like all people, I would rather dwell on successes instead of failures, and I would rather dwell on what's best with mankind instead of what's worst. I want to believe that inside all people have good hearts, although sometimes you must dig deep to find that goodness and it is often a struggle to get it out. Someone once wrote that true love is never easy, and neither is life. What we hope and pray for is that our presence here in Carries and on the planet, and with the presence of the Holy Spirit around us, makes life *easier* for all those we touch, for all those we come into contact with and for all those for whom we pray. We cannot change the whole world, but we can change a little part of it. Imagine the possibilities if each of us changed just a little part. If you think that is only wishful thinking, let me remind that Christianity started with Jesus and twelve simple guys, and that movement is now two billion strong with the power to move mountains.

TWENTY-NINE
The City of Grace

You would think that all stories have a beginning and an end, but this one does not. It has a beginning, certainly, and there is a stopping point, but if there is ever an end, with God's blessings it will be long after I've gone and far into the future after the mission has been completed.

† † †

I believe in divine appointments. I understand that no meeting is without God's involvement, but some are purposefully put together to make something great happen. I believe that Doodle came to us because God wanted it. And Fritz Meier with Gleanings. And there are others, too.

One important meeting came seemingly by mistake.

Someone I'd never met, Pastor Trimble, a bear of a man at 6 foot 3 inches tall, was traveling with a group of 18 others and the little troupe was hopelessly lost while looking for where they had an appointment for dinner. After passing by Ocean View a couple of times they pulled in and we gave him directions to where they needed to be, but after arriving at the destination the pastor left and returned to Ocean View. "I didn't like it there," he told me, so we fed him and put him up for the night. In the morning he said to me, "You must be a Christian to have treated me so well" and we laughed and talked over breakfast and into the morning about hopes and dreams and a little village that I felt had been touched by the power of God's hand.

His team had been working in Carrefour and he said to me, "I don't want to go to back Carrefour. I want to see what's going on *here*" so I took him across the highway that morning and I introduced him to our kids and I showed him a spot of land that I didn't know for what purpose it was to be used. The pastor looked into my eyes and said, "God is going to build the City of Grace here, Linotte." And as we looked out over the landscape he reminded me to always stay humble before adding, "God is going to make this an icon of Haiti," and we prayed for the land and he prayed for me.

Six months later the pastor came back with a big team and he's been coming twice a year ever since.

If there is a "City of Grace" idea, or vision, or revelation, it started up on the hill that morning with Pastor Trimble. I'm still not one-hundred percent sure what that even means, but we're working toward it anyway.

A group came to Ocean View for a week and on their last night they sat with the team and told about their experiences working at the mission. The eldest, a man who'd traveled the world, stated that of all the places he'd been to, and of all the mission trips he'd been on where great things were being attempted, it was his opinion that Mission of Grace had the best chance for long term success. That's all well and good, and nice to hear, but we can't rest on what we've done, we have to follow through with the promise of Jesus. We have done a lot, but more needs to be done. We can look back and take a deep breath, but we cannot rest. The forces that are continually at play to make places like the Mission of Grace unsuccessful *never* rest and if we are not moving forward then we are moving backward. There are a million ways for our mission to get sidetracked and it only takes one for all our victories to be swallowed up by the enemy who always seeks a crack in the armor and is always looking for a way to undermine God and God's people. That is what he does and he's been perfecting his battle for thousands of years, but God has been perfecting *His* battle, too, and with the mighty sword of Jesus, that battle will be won, in the mission, in Carries, and in Haiti.

I would not be telling the truth if I didn't admit to disappointments, many in fact, but there has never been abandonment. Even in my worst moments, that have been few in number, God has carried me far and has borne my uncertainties. And as we move forward and expand into the City of Grace, I feel I need to trust God even *more*, to let Him do His thing even if I can't understand the reason or purpose. I should not be anxious because I've never lifted a finger here, and I know what God's promise is, and if it's not here yet, then it's coming soon.

I am often asked if there is hope for Haiti, a place where hopelessness runs rampant. There is an old Haitian proverb that reads — *Piti piti zwazo fè nich li*, or, Little by little the bird makes his nest, and in essence, we are the bird and Carries is the nest. Little bit by little bit, the Mission of Grace *is* a model for what is capable of being done in the rest of the country. It's not easy, but nothing worth doing ever is, and it takes people who are willing to do what's right to be at the forefront of change. It also takes sacrifices that many aren't willing to make, and it takes belief that the work being done is righteous and good, but most importantly, it takes a mandate by God. Sometimes, not even the best thought-out plans are given the blessing of the Almighty and without that blessing success is not assured.

God only blesses you according to your heart, and Haiti's heart is a dark place where light can rarely be found. Blessings here are hard to come by and in order to receive the blessings God wants to pour down on us the heart must be set free. This is difficult to do in a place with a long history of defying God's orders, of praising false gods and where people's lives are centered on personal pleasures regardless of the cost to their soul or mind.

However, despite all that is, and all that has been, there *is* hope for Haiti. Nothing happens overnight and nothing happens without the intercession of the Holy Spirit.

Hope will come to Haiti a little bit at a time.

Hope will come to Haiti one child at a time.

If we stop believing that there is hope for Haiti, or for anyone anywhere, then we should stop calling ourselves Christians and find other ways to spend our time. That is a harsh assessment but what else did Jesus offer us but hope for an eternal life if we believe. Belief has wide arms and can stretch over whole countries—like Haiti.

The Mission of Grace has over a hundred employees and it is our desire that we not be simply a paycheck, but that those who work for us are also part of the historical future of Haiti. What we embrace, what we hold to be sacred, what we ask God for, are all tied together in a very untidy knot. We don't know what lies in the future, only God does, but we move toward that future with the belief that we've been blessed by God and that He will protect our endeavors. He knows what's in our hearts and in that knowledge we can attempt to be a shining example of a city upon a hill.

The 'shining city on the hill' motif is often used and rarely attained. That does not mean that we should stop reaching and seeking, but how do *we* as a mission get there?

We don't accept selfishness, but we seek selflessness.
Respect is to be a norm.

Giving of one's self in service is what the mission is based on.

Humbleness and humility are keys of the mission and of Christianity, for as Isaiah 1:17 states;

> Learn to do right; seek justice.
> Defend the oppressed.
> Take up the cause of the fatherless;
> plead the case of the widow.

God will never find fault with taking care of the orphans and widows and that is what we as a mission are commanded to do.

The Golden Rule is not just a Christian code, but a human attitude that has been all-too lacking in Haiti. Selfishness cannot be tolerated and disrespect needs to be bred out and replaced with respect that can spread like a wildfire.

It is not always easy to follow a Christian path, and it is often much easier to follow the ways of the enemy than it is to follow Jesus. Most importantly, it's easily forgotten that sin never ends well.

I am often asked what the future holds for the Mission of Grace and that is a difficult question to answer. In Creole we have a saying—*Nèg fè lide-l, Bondye ba-l dwa*, that is, 'Man gets the idea but God authorizes it.' Whatever plans or ideas I have, none of them are worth a whole lot if they aren't blessed by God. Some of what

I envision may never see the light of day because it is not a part of His plan. But for the purposes of *my* vision, what does the future hold for the Mission of Grace? A hospital, a larger orphanage, a much larger women's home, a secondary school, a church that will seat 700. The wish list and dream goes far beyond all that, too. I want to see 2,000 jobs created in the community. I want to see the mission self-reliant. I want to see businesses come here to Carries and I want to see investment that will serve us long term. Too often Haiti has looked at the quick fix and the solution that will be for now but not for the tomorrow. I want our solutions to be for *all* time.

Are all of those possible? It is possible to move mountains with God's blessing, so building a hospital should be a breeze, and what are 2,000 jobs to the Lord who has created *millions* of jobs?

We have done a lot, but we can do more. We have accepted the challenge that God planted in our hearts and in our brains and He doesn't do so unless He expects those challenges to be answered. We might stumble and fall, we might be burdened and troubled, and it certainly will not be easy, but nothing worth doing ever is. But with God as our guide to lead us through the troubled waters, all things are possible.

TO FIND OUT MORE

We are always happy to have visitors, be it groups or individuals, to come and volunteer in the mission. To learn more about the Mission of Grace, or to make a donation, visit our website at:

www.missionofgracehaiti.org